Please return this training resource to the Training and Development Department by the date shown.

REF:	
DATE BOOKED OUT	DATE TO BE RETURNED
26·11·12	30·1·12

Profiles in Performance

Profiles in Performance

Business Intelligence Journeys and the Roadmap for Change

HOWARD DRESNER

John Wiley & Sons, Inc.

Published by John Wiley & Sons, Inc., Hoboken, New Jersey.
Published simultaneously in Canada.

For general information on our other products and services or for technical
support, please contact our Customer Care Department within the United States at
(800) 762-2974, outside the United States at (317) 572-3993 or fax (317) 572-4002.

Wiley also publishes its books in a variety of electronic formats. Some content
that appears in print may not be available in electronic books. For more
information about Wiley products, visit our web site at www.wiley.com.

Library of Congress Cataloging-in-Publication Data:

Dresner, Howard, 1957-
Profiles in performance : business intelligence journeys and the roadmap for
change/Howard Dresner.
p. cm.
Includes bibliographical references and index.
ISBN 978-0-470-40886-5 (cloth)
1. Corporate culture–Case studies. 2. Organizational effectiveness–Case
studies. 3. Organizational behavior–Case studies. 4. Performance–Case
studies. 5. Management–Case studies. I. Title.
HD58.7.D764 2010
658.3′14–dc22

2009024940

Printed in the United States of America

10 9 8 7 6 5 4 3 2 1

To my wife, Patty, and to Sarah, and Hugh, and Joshua, and Ethan

Contents

Foreword

Performance management is frequently singled out as a standalone management program, often accompanied with acronyms like "CPM," "BPM," or "EPM." Performance management is more than a program; it is how organizations achieve goals through the concerted actions of others. You can make the case that performance management is the primary role of the management profession.

When we talk of performance management (PM), we frequently glamorize the results of successful companies—organizations like Procter & Gamble, Apple and IBM. Obviously, if they succeeded, they mastered PM. We also glamorize the means by which they succeeded—programs like Six Sigma or technologies like Business Intelligence. All too often, we take the role of the individual employee for granted. This is unfortunate, because at the end of the day, the only changes that are important are those activated by individuals—organization performance is the sum of individual performance.

In *Profiles in Performance*, Howard Dresner begins with the premise that "people trump processes and technology every time." He provides an interesting framework to think about change, arguing that performance improvements emanate from a "performance-directed culture." The model that he proposes describes how the institution can foster this culture by managing a set of strategic, operational and technical criteria. The framework is illustrated in a series of well documented case studies.

Howard Dresner is to be congratulated for raising awareness of the role of culture as the grass roots of performance
and for providing practical approaches to build this culture.
Hopefully, this book will not only be read but will be used by
professionals who want to create new levels of performance in
their organizations.

Dr. David P. Norton
Co-author, *The Balanced Scorecard*
Director, The Palladium Group

Preface

My previous book, *The Performance Management Revolution*, was about the coming revolution in performance management and my belief in the ascendancy of a new management system for the global enterprise in the 21st century.

Every business has a management system, but in my view, a modern management system consists of people, processes, and technologies aligned and optimized for performance. It empowers people to make decisions and take action on their own, defines processes for increasingly decentralized organizational structures, and uses technology to support people and processes day-to-day while providing a platform for long-term business growth.

As I began work on this book, my intention was to capture and present best practices for creating the management system I've just described. Along the way, I realized something essential to my task: Before an organization can succeed, it first must create a culture that values performance, transparency, and accountability. In other words, people trump processes and technology every time.

Intuitively, we know this is true. We've all worked in organizations where a technology initiative was scrapped or stalled because an important group of people didn't buy in: Senior management offered lukewarm support, managers felt that they had not been consulted enough in the design of the system, or the system was so complex that end users could not use it.

This does not mean that technology is not important. It is—but as an enabler of people, and not the other way around.

Slowly, over the past few decades, this point of view has become conventional wisdom in management expert circles. A 2008 McKinsey & Company article on how to make operational improvements last notes that many companies overlook up to half of the potential benefits of such efforts because they underestimate either the level of senior management involvement required or the potential of employee "mind-sets" to undermine them, or both.[1] Here's what that says to me: You can have the best technology in the world and it won't help you if your culture is working against you.

These realizations prompted me to shift the focus of this book to people and culture, and to organizations that have established—or have made enough progress that there is no turning back—from what I call a performance-directed culture.

Energized by this new focus, I decided that before I could begin interviewing organizations and considering them as candidates for case studies, I needed a model that would provide a lens or filter through which I could assess their culture. That led me to develop the Performance Culture Maturity Model ™, which I will explore in depth in the first chapter of this book and refer to many times throughout in the case studies that are presented here.

The Maturity Model is the most comprehensive model of its kind that I am aware of. It helps me understand the path specific organizations have taken in their quest for better performance. It also allows me to position an organization along that path at specific points in time, and that is valuable too. If there is

---

[1] David Fine, Maia A. Hanson, and Stefan Roggenhofer, "From Lean to Lasting: Making Operational Improvements Stick," *The McKinsey Quarterly* (November 2008).

one thing I have learned in the course of my career, it's that a performance-directed culture is a journey, not a destination.

I also believe that it will be a useful tool for you—as a student or practitioner of performance management—because it will help you to assess your own organization's strengths and weaknesses, accomplishments, and challenges—and create an action plan to improve.

The Maturity Model certainly helped me select organizations for the four case studies in this book: The Denihan Hospitality Group, a growing hotel management and development company based in New York City; Cleveland, Ohio-based Cleveland Clinic, one of the largest and most innovative health systems in the world; Northern California Public Broadcasting, based in San Francisco and parent company to the most-watched and most-listened to public media stations in the country; and Mueller Inc., a leading provider of pre-engineered metal building and residential metal roofing products headquartered in the Central West Texas town of Ballinger.

As diverse as these organizations are geographically, in the products and services they deliver, and the constituents they serve, they share a common goal: to build and sustain a performance-directed culture.

Here is another distinctive feature of this book. Classic case studies present a problem, a solution, and results—giving rather more air time to the starting point and the outcomes than to the details of what transpires in between. This book will take you inside what happens in organizations striving to build a performance-directed culture—the good, the bad, and the ugly. The task is not easy; the path is rarely clear; and every organization has its share of setbacks as well as successes. We can learn from both.

So what is a performance-directed culture? At the highest level, a performance-directed culture is one where everyone is actively aligned with the mission of the organization, where transparency and accountability are the norm, new insights are acted upon in unison, and conflicts are resolved positively and effectively. While this may sound like a Utopian world, there are organizations that have made great strides toward its achievement.

Here are some of them ... and their stories.

Howard Dresner
October 2009

Acknowledgments

I am deeply grateful to a number of colleagues, friends, and family whose contributions made this book possible.

I especially want to thank my collaborator, Susan Thomas. A superb researcher, writer, and thinking partner, Susan brought her own unique perspective and storytelling expertise to these case studies. The result is a book that is richer in content and was more enjoyable to write than it would have been without her.

At every organization we visited, many people generously gave us their time and freely shared their experiences. A few people worked tirelessly to ensure that we had access to the right individuals and information in a timely way. At the Denihan Hospitality Group, I owe special thanks to Brooke Barrett and Menka Uttamchandani. At Cleveland Clinic, I would like to acknowledge Tom Wadsworth, Chris Donovan, and Andrew Proctor. I am grateful to Jeff Nemy at KQED. At Mueller, I especially appreciate the efforts of Mark Lack and Bryan Davenport.

I would also like to thank the many people who offered insights into specific organizations as potential case study subjects. Meg Dussault, Dana Dye, Tom Nather, and Kathryn Whitmore were especially helpful.

I owe a debt to David Norton, best known as co-creator with Robert Kaplan of the Balanced Scorecard, for the Foreword to this book.

Thanks to my editors at Wiley, Tim Burgard, and Stacey Rivera, who once again offered valuable feedback and encouragement.

To Patty, my wife of 27 years, whose love, patience, and support sustain me each and every day.

And, to my daughter, Sarah, son-in-law Hugh, and sons, Joshua and Ethan—all extraordinary people that I am very fortunate to have in my life.

CHAPTER 1

Performance-Directed Culture

What is a performance-directed culture and how can you tell when an organization has achieved it? These were the essential questions facing me when I developed my Performance Culture Maturity Model™.

To help answer this question, I developed six criteria—shown here at the top of the model in Figure 1.1—with four levels of maturity (shown down the left side) that determine the degree to which an organization has made progress.

Four Levels of Maturity

The four levels of maturity determine how mature an organization is in each of six performance-directed culture criteria. Even the least mature organization would not be at the absolute lowest level in each category (I hope). So almost without exception, every enterprise will be at different levels of maturity across the six criteria. This is normal and is part of the process of assessing and improving an organization's maturity.

A technique used with our case study candidates (and others since) was to have them pick three dates and plot them on the Maturity Model, with the midpoint representing the moment when significant and positive changes toward

	Alignment with Mission	Transparency and Accountability	Action on Insights	Conflict Resolution	Common Trust in Data	Availability and Currency of Information
Performance-Directed Culture Realized	Actionable and embraced mission—supported, informed, and reinforced by metrics	General transparency and accountability accepted as cultural tenets	"Closed loop" processes ensure timely, concerted action	Established and effective mechanisms for resolving conflicts	Data as truth: Common application of data, filters, rules, and semantics	Currency of metrics/data matches rhythm of business
Performance-Directed Culture Emerging	Actionable mission supported by "top-down" metrics	Limited transparency and accountability; multiple functions collaborate	Ad hoc (informal) action on insights across functions	When identified, conflicts resolved on an impromptu basis	Common data: Provincial views and semantics used to support specific positions	Enterprise availability, uneven currency of information
Departmental Optimization	Alignment with discrete functional goals, not enterprise mission	Fragmented transparency and accountability within discrete functions	Uncoordinated/ parochial action (sometimes at the expense of others)	Appearance of cooperation, "opportunistic reconciliation"	Conflicting, functional views of data cause confusion, disagreement	Availability and currency directed by departmental sources
Chaos Reigns	Mission not actionable, not communicated, and/or not understood	Arbitrary accountability, general opacity	Insights rarely leveraged	Conflicting, redundant, and competing efforts are the norm	Data and information generally unreliable and distrusted	Multiple, inconsistent data sources, conflicting semantics

FIGURE 1.1 Performance Culture Maturity Model™

Source: Copyright 2009 - Patent Pending - Dresner Advisory Services, LLC

becoming a performance-directed culture began to emerge. The first date is some earlier date—before enlightenment—and the third date is where they are today. Not only was this approach useful to help better understand today's strengths and weaknesses, and accomplishments and areas for improvement, but it gave me an understanding of the chronology of key events, and the cause and effect relationships (see Figure 1.2).

Level One: Chaos Reigns

The first and lowest level of achievement on the Maturity Model is Chaos Reigns. At this level, little progress or achievement toward a performance-directed culture is evident. Fragmentation and disorganization are the norm. This is not a sustainable state, with organizations at this level at serious risk of collapse.

One colleague of mine suggested that a more politically correct term for this level might be "dysfunction." However, I'm not sure that's much of an improvement. Another colleague suggested that this should be called performance-directed culture "hell." I'm more inclined to agree with him. Assuming that there was an organization stuck at this level across all categories, it would be a very unpleasant place to work—as an employee, partner, or customer. Regardless of what you choose to call it, there's no place to go from here but up.

Level Two: Departmental Optimization

The next level of achievement is called Departmental Optimization. At this level, departments and functions are playing for themselves. While this sort of organization seems to function well enough to survive, cooperation and collaboration are virtually unheard of. Management is either ineffective or uninterested

	Alignment with Mission	Transparency and Accountability	Action on Insights	Conflict Resolution	Common Trust in Data	Availability and Currency of Information
Performance-Directed Culture Realized	Actionable and embraced mission—supported, informed, and reinforced by metrics [2007/9]	General transparency and accountability accepted as cultural tenets [2007/9]	"Closed loop" processes ensure timely, concerted action	Established and effective mechanisms for resolving conflicts [2009]	Data as truth: Common [2009] application of data, filters, rules, and semantics	Currency of metrics/data matches rhythm of business [2007/9]
Performance-Directed Culture Emerging	Actionable mission supported by "top-down" metrics [2005/6]	Limited [2005/6] transparency and accountability; multiple functions collaborate [2003/4]	Ad hoc (informal) action on insights [2005/6] across functions [2007/9]	When identified, conflicts resolved on an impromptu basis [2007/8]	Common data: Provincial views and semantics used to support specific positions [2007/8]	Enterprise availability, uneven currency of information [2005/6]
Departmental Optimization	Alignment with discrete functional goals, not enterprise [2000 mission] [2003/4]	Fragmented transparency and accountability within discrete functions [2003/4] [2000]	Uncoordinated/ parochial action (sometimes at the expense of others) [2003/4] [2000]	Appearance of cooperation, "opportunistic reconciliation" [2005/6] [2003/4] [2000]	Conflicting, functional views of data cause [2000] confusion, [2003/4] disagreement [2005/6]	Availability and currency [2003/4] directed by departmental sources [2000] [2005/6]
Chaos Reigns	Mission not actionable, not communicated, and/or not understood	Arbitrary accountability, general opacity	Insights rarely leveraged	Conflicting, redundant, and competing efforts are the norm	Data and information generally unreliable and distrusted	Multiple, inconsistent data sources, conflicting semantics

FIGURE 1.2 Performance Culture Maturity Model™ with examples of dates

Source: Copyright 2009 - Patent Pending - Dresner Advisory Services, LLC

in forging alignment with its mission or fostering cooperation across functions.

Oddly enough, this is the most common level for organizations and it raises an important point about our human nature. Humans have always favored working in small groups of people with similar backgrounds, outlooks, and goals. Anthropologists refer to these groups as tribes. Historically, tribes were small bands of related kinfolk who worked together for basic survival. If we look around today, we can see these sorts of tribes in modern society and in business. For example, we can think of corporate departments and functions as tribes of a sort. With similar backgrounds and experiences, outlooks and goals, they work together to protect their tribe from outside threats.

Hence we have the Finance tribe, the Human Resources tribe, the Sales tribe, and so on, with each of these either covertly competing against the others or in direct conflict. While this sort of behavior may be a good match for our natural human programming, it's not particularly helpful for the greater enterprise.

Level Three: Performance-Directed Culture Emerging

At the level of Performance-Directed Culture Emerging, an organization has started to see the benefits of working across departmental barriers and is more focused upon a common mission. Cross-functional sharing and cooperation tend to be impromptu and opportunistic. Two or more functions may start to work together for mutual benefit. Word of mouth of their success starts to spread. A virtuous cycle is starting to emerge as the benefits of a performance-directed culture become obvious, with management providing the needed support and encouragement.

This is what I consider the point of no return, where an organization inevitably will achieve a fully mature performance-directed culture, given time. It should be noted that, from my experience, it is difficult to begin to reach this level without a profound (and positive) change on the part of an organization's leadership. This sort of change usually is associated with a physical change of management, in favor of more enlightened leadership, or a major event that serves as a wake-up call for existing management.

Level Four: Performance-Directed Culture Realized

By the level of Performance-Directed Culture Realized, performance improvement has permeated the very fabric of an organization's culture. Processes center around transparency and accountability. Individuals are rewarded for sharing, cooperating, and supporting the mission of the enterprise. The enterprise thinks, strategizes, plans, analyzes, and executes as a single organism. In Maslow's world, this would be the equivalent of "self-actualization."

Before we all start feeling like failures, you should know that I have not yet found this perfect organization. It may exist. But if it does, it's well hidden. However, the performance-directed cultures I have observed often have some of their attributes at these lofty levels. So, just as we can think of a performance-directed culture as more of a journey than a destination, we also can think of the achievement of perfection as less important than its pursuit.

It should come as no surprise that organizations that have achieved a good measure of performance-directed culture (levels three and four) are great companies to work for and do business with. As I spent more time with the case study organizations in this book, I couldn't help thinking what interesting and fun places they must be to work at. These organizations are positive and purposeful, with motivated employees and delighted customers—some more than others, of course.

Six Performance-Directed Culture Criteria

Each of my six performance-directed culture criteria falls into one of three categories: strategic, operational, or technical, as shown in Figure 1.3.

In the strategic category are Alignment with Mission and Transparency and Accountability. Because they are strategic, these attributes must be initiated and driven—or at the very least recognized and actively supported—by the most senior of management, typically C-level executives.

In the operational category are Action on Insights and Conflict Resolution. Operational criteria are something everyone in an organization has a role in driving on a day-to-day basis.

In the technical category are Common Trust in Data and Availability and Currency of Information. Technical criteria are managed in partnership between business management and the IT function or other technical resources.

Strategic Criteria

Strategic criteria are driven and controlled by the most senior levels of management. That's to say that no other level within the organization can raise the organization up to the levels of

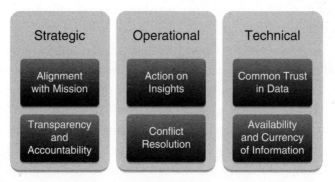

FIGURE 1.3 Performance-Directed Culture Criteria

a performance-directed culture for these two criteria: Alignment with Mission, and Transparency and Accountability. Additionally, these two criteria will help elevate all other areas of performance-directed culture achievement. It's also worth noting that without them, a true performance-directed culture is not attainable.

ALIGNMENT WITH MISSION   Before we can talk about Alignment with Mission, it's important to have a viable mission statement. Of course, that begs the question: "What makes for a good mission statement?" I'm not going to spend a great deal of time on this point, since there are many books that do a better job than I can. However, I believe that the best mission statements are the simple ones that communicate what an organization is really about and that everyone can understand and rally around.

In the process, I looked at the mission statements for the Fortune 500 and was shocked at how bad many of them are. For example, if you need 100 words or more to describe it, you've missed the point. In fact, in reading most of them it's practically impossible to learn what these companies actually do. All too many of them talk about shareholder value or being the leader, serving their community or being the best. Many of them even reference profitability—which (hopefully) is one outcome of a good mission, not the mission itself. These mission statements are not ones that people in an organization can relate to or align with easily.

In contrast, others have created simple, meaningful, and actionable mission statements. For example, CVS's mission statement as presented on its web site is: "We will be the easiest pharmacy retailer for customers to use." It's clear and concise and everyone ought to know how to align with this idea. The mission statement communicated to me in interviews at Cleveland Clinic (see Chapter 3 for the case study) is "patient first." Once again, it's clear and concise and easy to align with.

A colleague of mine joined the employment of a large Latin American media company to help it with its enterprise-wide performance management initiative, and the first thing he asked of his new boss—the CIO—was: "What's our mission statement?" (This is a perfectly reasonable question, in my opinion.) The CIO didn't know and, apparently, had never thought to ask for himself. Now curious, he posited the question to his management. The question went all the way to the CEO, who assured him that the company did have one, and a good one to boot. However, he couldn't share it because—and this is the funny part—it was a secret! Imagine that! A secret mission statement!

To be effective—it should go without saying—a mission statement has to be shared openly and communicated throughout the organization. The best mission statement is of no use if it's a secret. So, with that in mind, let's look at the four levels of maturity for Alignment with Mission.

Alignment with Mission: Level One   Level one is the lowest stage of achievement for Alignment with the Mission. Here the mission is either not viable, not actionable, not communicated, and/or not understood. Our example of the secret mission statement fits nicely into this category. Also in this category are those mission statements that try to associate the enterprise with whatever is hot at the moment or that will create a positive image for the public, but don't tell you who the organization is or what it actually does. So, to be effective and to foster a performance-directed culture, a mission statement can't be extracurricular, for example, endorse corporate social responsibility, be green, and so on. In other words, it has to describe what the company really does and truly stands for.

Alignment with Mission: Level Two   While there might be an enterprise mission, at this level it often is overlooked in favor of alignment with discrete functional goals within departments.

Whether intentional or unintentional, explicit or implicit, these departments have developed their own mission and drive departmental alignment within it. While they may pay lip service to a corporate mission, the reality is quite different. Discrete departmental missions may overlap with peer departmental missions. Indeed, management of each may be consciously working to expand their mission and conquer other areas of responsibility and authority for their own parochial gain.

Alignment with Mission: Level Three   At this level a proper and actionable mission has been defined and communicated from the top down. Companies at this level know who they are, know their strengths and weaknesses, and have a strategy and a drive to improve. Through strong leadership, employees (and other stakeholders) have embraced and internalized the mission. There is a clear understanding, at a personal, departmental, divisional, and enterprise level, about what it means to support and align with this mission. Appropriate plans and top-down metrics have been created and pushed downward to support and reinforce alignment. However, organizational observations and experience don't reliably inform and influence strategy in a bidirectional way. This creates the potential for placing the vision and strategy out of sync with the ever-changing operational business environment.

Alignment with Mission: Level Four   As with the level above, there's a solid mission statement with alignment (and ownership) throughout the organization and across all stakeholders. However, the major difference at this level is that observations, insights, and ideas from below filter back up to management to inform, influence, and mold the strategy—better ensuring support for the mission—as the external (and internal) environment changes.

TRANSPARENCY AND ACCOUNTABILITY   Funny thing about Transparency and Accountability: Everyone says it's important and everyone is (publicly) in favor of it. Yet, both are very hard to achieve in almost every organization. Seems like a contradiction, doesn't it? But in fact, it isn't. Here's why.

What people mean when they claim support for Transparency and Accountability is the following: They want everyone to be transparent with them while they remain opaque, and they want others to be held accountable without being held accountable themselves. In contrast, real transparency means that everyone openly and freely shares information with others, including information about their own performance. In a transparent and accountable organization, metrics have a clear cause and effect relationship and everyone has the information and tools to control their own performance—in harmony with others, not at their expense. Accordingly, we hold ourselves, and one another, accountable for performance—individually and collectively.

Transparency and Accountability: Level One   At this stage of achievement, there is no real transparency. Knowledge is power and few are willing to relinquish that power—even if the enterprise will benefit. Typically, the only way to know what's really going on is to have a personal information network, with people in the know willing to help.

Accountability is not based on real or tangible plans and is not aligned with a larger, enterprise-wide (or even departmental) mission. Instead, it is dependent on local or immediate management and their ideals, biases, and, sometimes, private agendas. As a result, what people are held accountable for will change. So, goals and objectives (and measures) agreed upon at the beginning of the year may not be used to measure people at the end of the year.

While this may sound insidious, it can be quite innocent. For example, at the beginning of the year, an employee and his or her manager may agree on goals, which may include things like customer satisfaction, quality, efficiency, revenue, and profitability. However, due to the opacity of the organization, at the end of the year, measurement might be limited to whatever reliable information is available—perhaps only revenue. Of course, over time, employees get wise to this and focus only on those metrics they are certain will be used to measure them.

In previous roles, I've personally observed this sort of dynamic. And, it was always interesting to watch new associates struggle (against good advice) to achieve all of the goals and objectives laid out early in the year only to learn (much too late) that revenue was the only goal that really mattered.

Transparency and Accountability: Level Two   At this level, it is not uncommon to find departments within an enterprise that share information and are held accountable only within their function, by immediate management and peers, but are closed and opaque to everyone else in the enterprise. Typically, a departmental mission is the driving force behind this sort of Transparency and Accountability. Any mandatory sharing of information or shared accountability is done in the narrowest way possible to maintain secrecy and protect territorial boundaries. And, in many cases, a department will skew information to better position itself or obstruct other (competitive) functions. This lack of Transparency and Accountability often is used to shift the blame for failure.

Transparency and Accountability: Level Three   At this stage, limited Transparency and Accountability begin to emerge, with multiple functions beginning to collaborate. While this may start opportunistically—with cooperating groups leveraging one another for self-serving purposes—the benefits of sharing, openness, and collaboration start to become apparent. Information sharing expands and eventually leads to shared metrics across functions. However, at this point, there is still no overarching corporate initiative, with much of the organization still operating at lower levels.

Transparency and Accountability: Level Four   At this level, general Transparency and Accountability are accepted and embraced as cultural tenets and are part of the corporate fabric. The open sharing of information, insights, and ideas is encouraged and rewarded. Shared metrics are the norm, with users finding new ways to improve their collective performance and that of the enterprise.

Operational Criteria

The criteria in this category are unique in that management cannot control or direct them. This is the realm of every person. The rank-and-file employees and stakeholders determine how and when to execute against these criteria. Hence, success or failure is in their hands. Because of their operational nature, these criteria represent continuous processes, which require constant attention and diligence to avoid regression to a previous stage.

ACTION ON INSIGHTS   Of course, the old adage, that information is power, comes to mind. However, to be more accurate, I would change information to insight. But, first let's define insight.

The Wiktionary definition of insight is: "the power of acute observation and deduction, penetration, discernment, perception."

To my way of thinking, insight is meaningful information, with context, that enables a person to develop perspective and understanding, making the underlying information both relevant and actionable. And, it needn't come from an information system. It can come from any source. And, by action, I mean the ability to effect change as a result of leveraging that insight for the benefit of an individual and/or organization.

Action on Insights: Level One   At this level there simply isn't much insight to act on. Individuals rely upon intuition and instincts to make decisions, and have a limited understanding of the issues facing them. The resulting decision-making process is little better than guessing. In the event that a real insight is stumbled upon, it may be leveraged for some personal advantage. But, more than likely, its potential benefit will never be realized.

Action on Insights: Level Two   At this level, insights are leveraged and perspective developed in alignment with a departmental mission. These insights and the resulting departmental action may take place at the expense of a peer department. A perfect example is when two product/business groups identify a market opportunity and both develop products/services to address it—effectively competing in the market with each other.

Action on Insights: Level Three   At this level insights are shared across two or more departments and actions also may be coordinated, but on a somewhat opportunistic basis. However, this is the beginning of performance-directed culture behavior, where more-concerted action is becoming more common. Still, enterprise-wide processes for acting on insights have not yet emerged.

Action on Insights: Level Four   At this level enterprise processes have been established to help drive a coordinated and concerted response to insights. For example, if Marketing learns something valuable about a target market, it may translate that insight into a new campaign. The plan surrounding this campaign will include collaboration with Sales, Manufacturing, Finance,

Distribution, Human Resources, and so on. It's a holistic plan that is vetted and executed in unison. Changes during execution are shared and the entire organization, and its shared plan, evolves until it hits its stride. In this scenario, nobody is blindsided and there are few surprises. Surprises that do emerge are dealt with quickly. And, early successes are quickly amplified before the opportunity passes.

CONFLICT RESOLUTION   Conflict is a part of human nature. We all come with different experiences, perspectives, goals, and objectives. However, conflict can be a positive force. By vetting multiple opinions in an open and constructive fashion, a more complete and thoughtful solution to a problem can be created, with greater inclusion and camaraderie. Or, it can be negative—with opinions held secretly and passive-aggressive behavior as the norm. Conflicting perspectives, semantics, and outlooks inevitably manifest themselves as competing projects, products, or functions.

Conflict Resolution: Level One   In organizations at this level, dissenting opinions, although certainly present, are not openly aired. Management is unwilling to challenge itself to resolve differing perspectives and attitudes. Instead, it allows them to fester—manifesting themselves as contradictions within the organization and the business.

Early in my career, I worked for a large organization where management allowed the creation of competing efforts, under the guise that it was healthy for the organization. The result was employees were pitted against one another with the knowledge that those who lost the competition also might lose their jobs and livelihoods. You can imagine what sort of environment this created. Conflict was the norm. In fact, it was all-out warfare. In the final analysis, this company (which no longer exists) would have fared better had it fostered a culture of cooperation and conflict resolution. So, while this sort of cutthroat environment is rare, there is a bit of it in many organizations.

Conflict Resolution: Level Two   At this level management weighs in on some important issues and drives the resolution of some conflicts (or tries to). Sometimes it succeeds but often it merely creates the illusion of reconciliation. Conflicting views typically are not aired. Private agendas still abound—with only limited conflicts grudgingly resolved.

Conflict Resolution: Level Three   Management has begun to create an environment where it is safe and encouraged to exchange differing points of view. When identified, conflicts get resolved on an impromptu basis. In this scenario, people are less likely to purposely create conflict. Nevertheless, there are no consistent, enterprise-wide mechanisms for resolving conflict. Instead, individuals, when they encounter potentially conflicting efforts, must develop their own process for resolution. Accordingly, the quality of the outcome will vary from case to case.

Conflict Resolution: Level Four   At this level dissenting voices are encouraged and included as vital in the decision-making processes of the organization. For major undertakings, management requires that they be vetted to ensure that they don't conflict with other efforts. In this way, conflict is avoided before major investments are made. Of course, conflict cannot be avoided entirely. Instead, in this scenario, the organization has established a best-practice set of protocols for identifying and resolving conflict in a way that is both positive and most beneficial for the enterprise. Unlike my example where the losing group might forfeit their jobs, in this situation competing efforts might be combined—leveraging the strengths of each to create a single initiative that is stronger than either would have been independently.

Technical Criteria

Although a performance-directed culture is not driven by technology, certain aspects of technology are important enablers. In particular, the availability, currency, and trust in data are absolutely critical for a performance-directed culture to be created and sustained in the long term and on an enterprise-wide scale. So, in acknowledgment of this reality, I included two criteria that focus upon information technology—specifically, data. Although data warehousing and Business Intelligence (BI) technologies play a role here, they must be employed in alignment with the other performance-directed culture criteria: strategy and operations.

COMMON TRUST IN DATA   For a performance-directed culture to thrive, it must be supported by reliable information whose veracity is ensured and widely accepted. This information serves as the substrate on which all decisions are framed and made in a performance-directed culture. Developing and delivering a trusted data environment is extremely difficult work—not because of technology, but because of the reluctance of people to have faith in and rely upon it. It can take many years to build such a reputation and only an instant to destroy it.

Common Trust in Data: Level One   In this scenario, data is more likely to misinform than inform. Instead, people rely on other, more informal, sources of information or they rely upon experience or intuition (better known as guessing) or anecdotal information from colleagues or various publications.

Common Trust in Data: Level Two   In this scenario, data is available and (generally) trusted within specific functions, for example, Finance. However, differing views of data, as supported by various stove-piped systems, cannot be easily reconciled.

Management frustration with this status quo may lead to an IT-driven data warehouse project—without resolving the underlying business conditions that created irreconcilable data views.

Common Trust in Data: Level Three   In this scenario, a common and reliable source of data is in place and its veracity is generally accepted. However, some will apply varying filters and semantics to better position themselves, their departments, or their projects. As a performance-directed culture emerges, this sort of behavior will be rejected as unacceptable and will dissipate.

Common Trust in Data: Level Four   At this point, the organization has a trusted information source that is not disputed or manipulated for parochial purposes. Managers arrive at meetings collectively briefed on relevant information and come prepared to address presenting problems. Debate about the data is at a minimum.

AVAILABILITY AND CURRENCY OF INFORMATION   The Availability and Currency of Information contribute greatly to developing trust in the data. By availability, I mean completeness of the information (as many sources as needed) to build a useful business perspective. Availability also means that the information must be accessible whenever the business needs it. By currency, I mean that the freshness and periodicity must match the needs of the business. For example, the business may require certain metrics or key performance indicators to be reported as weekly indicators, but updated daily.

Availability and Currency of Information: Level One   At this level the information sources are in chaos. Reports generated by operational systems provide a limited view of reality and offer a poor rearview mirror analysis of the business. Users are forced to piece data together by themselves—often causing the use and proliferation of spreadsheet technology and what I like to call micro-marts of data. The resulting spreadsheet models are shared, modified, and shared again. I often liken this to the game of telephone we played as children. The first child whispers a phrase to the next child, and so on, until the end where the final phrase bears little resemblance to the original one.

Availability and Currency of Information: Level Two At this level, departmental systems provide a good and consistent view of the function's operations and business. However, each department and function has its own discrete systems and outlook on the world, making it difficult to reconcile them for a more complete enterprise view. When required by management to provide a more complete view, people must expend tremendous amounts of energy—only to deliver a flawed perspective, much too late.

Availability and Currency of Information: Level Three At this level the enterprise has excellent availability of information that is of good quality and complete. However, the currency of the information may not be consistently aligned with the needs of the business.

Availability and Currency of Information: Level Four At this level, the currency of metrics and data matches the rhythm of the business. In this instance the information is as complete as possible, quality and integrity of data are outstanding, and the periodicity and currency are a perfect match to the business requirements.

The Maturity Model as an Assessment Tool

While I created the Performance Culture Maturity Model to filter and select case studies for this book, it should serve as a tool to assess and chart your own progress toward becoming a performance-directed culture. Remember that no organization gets top marks for all six criteria and that progress in one area may cause you to temporarily regress in another area. However, by using this tool, you can determine strengths and weaknesses as well as areas on which to focus your efforts near and long term. The model also can be used to conduct regular pre- and post-project assessments in order to recognize and acknowledge areas for improvement to maintain momentum.

CHAPTER 2

Denihan Hospitality Group

If you're looking for examples of companies creating a performance-directed culture, one of the last places you might think to look is at a 50-year-old, family-owned business. In the case of Denihan Hospitality Group (DHG), you'd be wrong.

Headquartered in New York City, DHG's origins date back to 1962, when Benjamin Denihan, Sr., founded Manhattan East Suite Hotels (MESH) to serve long-term visitors to the city with apartment-like hotel rooms. This was not the family's first business venture. In the early 1900s, Denihan's parents started a laundry and dry cleaning business that became known as the "Cleaners to the Stars" because of an exclusive client list that included the Vanderbilt family, Hattie Carnegie, and later, Marilyn Monroe. Denihan built Manhattan East Suite Hotels' first hotel—Affinia Gardens—on East 64th Street on the site of his family's laundry and dry cleaning business.

In 1985, the company repositioned to capitalize on a new trend in the hotel industry—the all-suite hotel, catering to business travelers. The company was already well established in this business—at the time, it owned all nine of the city's all-suite hotels—and when Denihan died in 1986, the company was New York's largest owner-operator of all-suite hotels.

Under Denihan, the company had prospered. His commitment to customer service was legendary, and by many accounts he was also a strong, determined, and detail-oriented business-man with a clear view of what he wanted to achieve and how to do it.

One decision he made that served the company well was to develop a shared services model for his hotels, centralizing support services to a greater degree than was standard practice in the hotel business. In addition to hotel functions such as finance, marketing, and sales, Denihan also centralized housekeeping and laundry—services that most hotel properties managed locally. Not only did this provide an economy of scale for Manhattan East Suite Hotels that enabled it to achieve margins above the industry standard for hotel companies of its type, but it also gave Denihan a greater degree of control over the day-to-day operations of each of his individual hotels, which was important to him.

Company lore has it that Denihan was so intent on maintaining tight control over his business operations and information about their performance that he personally drove the company's housekeepers to the hotels each morning. The number of house-keepers a hotel deploys each day is an indicator of its occupancy rates, and Denihan apparently didn't want anyone else privy to that information.

When Denihan died, ownership of the company passed to an equal partnership of six family members, but with no clear succession plan. Brooke Barrett—Denihan's daughter and one of the partners—has been quoted as saying of that time, "For the first year, we were basically frozen. Who was running the business? What were everyone's roles and responsibilities? Gradually we realized that we needed to sit down, plan, and move forward."[1]

---

[1] Staff Report, *New York Enterprise Report* (July/August 2007).

To their credit, the six partners worked it out, gradually settling into new and defined roles in the business and coming together as a group to make all key decisions. The company continued to achieve impressive (if measured) success and even launched a new luxury brand, The Benjamin — named for the founder Benjamin Denihan—and opened the first Benjamin-branded hotel in 1999.

9/11 Rocks the World

On September 11, 2001, terrorists hijacked four jet liners and crashed two of them into the twin towers of the World Trade Center in New York City, causing them to collapse and killing thousands of people. The shockwaves of 9/11 were felt around the world, with the United States and much of the developed world plunging into geopolitical and economic turmoil.

Not surprisingly, the New York hotel industry was especially hard hit. Typically a high-occupancy city, New York saw its occupancy rates plummet from more than 75 percent to just over 60 percent in September 2001, according to a report on selected post-9/11 economic indicators published in September 2003 by the Partnership for New York City. Because of its focus on long-term stays, MESH saw its occupancy percentage fall less than that of city hotels as a whole. Its mix of business changed dramatically, but MESH ran a 75 percent occupancy rate even in the fourth quarter of 2001.

The company also had made a decision previously that was to make an enormous difference in its ability to recover from the devastating effects of 9/11. Since 1997, the company had been collecting detailed data about its guests; however, it had not yet organized the data and/or produced reports that could help the six partners understand its significance and, even more importantly, make better business decisions based on insights from the data.

In 2000, Brooke Barrett—who was still just one of six equal partners—and then-Chief Information Officer John Cahill decided that it was time to put that data to work. They persuaded the other five partners that the company should launch a Business Intelligence (BI) initiative, hire a BI expert and invest in technology to support it.

Cahill had joined MESH in 1999 after an already distinguished technology career in the hotel business, including 16 years with The Sheraton Corporation and 14 years at Inter-Continental Hotels & Resorts. An inductee into the International Hospitality Hall of Fame, he served as the company's CIO for 10 years before retiring in May 2009. After a lengthy search for what Cahill calls "the right fit," in early 2001 the company hired Menka Uttamchandani from Hyatt International's Asia Pacific regional headquarters in Hong Kong—an expert in both BI and database marketing, with a proven track record of harnessing customer data to support decision making. Uttamchandani is DHG's Director of Business Intelligence.

Coming from a highly structured environment common in large and successful worldwide hotel chains, Uttamchandani was attracted to MESH by the opportunity to play a leadership role in helping a much smaller company in transition figure out how to use data rather than intuition to drive decisions, and to work across functional areas. She started her new job in April 2001.

"John and Brooke both had the strong belief that the company had all this valuable information but that it was disorganized and unstructured, and therefore could not be relied upon," says Uttamchandani. "And it was true: The data we had was amazing, going back to 1997, but we couldn't use it because we had no practical way to access and understand it—for example, we were using Excel to manually produce reports. I spent my first few months sorting through exactly what we had, figuring out how to improve its accuracy and integrity, and then organizing the data so we could design and deliver reports on the data that I felt could have the biggest impact on the business."

Because of the newness of the BI effort and a desire to move forward in a way that everyone in the company could appreciate, the company made another decision that turned out to be important in the wake of 9/11. Uttamchandani would focus initially on sales and marketing initiatives—and specifically on the customer data so that it could be mined to drive more revenue.

Says Uttamchandani: "The events of 9/11 totally threw our business—just as they did for everyone else. But because we had good customer data, we were able to immediately start using it in a smart, strategic way."

For example, many of the travelers still coming to New York City in the weeks following 9/11 were government employees, consultants, attorneys, and so on—after first responders, the people most involved in the early 9/11 investigative and recovery efforts. MESH had detailed information on its previous guests by industry and occupation, and was gratified to discover that a substantial percentage of its guests fit the profile of the people still coming to New York.

In addition, the company had detailed information on the preferences and behavior of guests in this category, for example, what services and amenities were most important to them during their stays and what types of promotions had worked to attract them in the past. As a result, the company was able to precisely focus its sales and marketing dollars on previous guests who were among those most likely to need hotel accommodations in New York City in the last few months of 2001 and into 2002. With very specific and highly targeted marketing campaigns aimed at people already in its database, MESH was able to significantly outperform its peers in attracting guests in the weeks and months after 9/11.

Following 9/11, this smart and aggressive use of historical information about previous guests, combined with creative marketing, transformed the status of data at MESH from a nice-to-have business tool to a crucial factor in the company's survival after 9/11. It also gave new momentum to the company's fledging BI initiative.

A New Era of Growth Begins

While 2002 was largely a year of recovery for MESH—as it was for all hotels in New York City—2003 marked the beginning of a new era of growth as the company began to execute on a decision to expand both in and outside of New York City. As part of that effort, in 2003 the company rebranded as Affinia Hospitality and launched its Affinia brand, billed by the company as a collection of "lifestyle hotels," each with its own special focus. The Affinia Dumont, the first Affinia-branded hotel, also opened in Manhattan in 2003 with an emphasis on fitness and wellness.

At the same time, the company's BI initiative also was expanding. Still primarily focused on sales and marketing, Uttamchandani supported several highly successful marketing campaigns, but also supported the company's expansion planning efforts. To help with the latter effort, for example, Uttamchandani gathered and analyzed data from existing guests about cities other than New York where they were traveling, where they stayed while there, and whether they would be open to staying in an Affinia hotel in those cities instead. This data was used to identify cities where Affinia Hospitality already had a loyal customer following and that therefore might be good candidates for expansion.

Uttamchandani also supported new efforts designed to increase revenue in existing properties with campaigns targeted at specific customer segments. One analytics project mined high-value guests who had broken their pattern of returning to the hotel within a certain period of time. The project focused on individual guests with a lifetime value of $20,000 or more, probing why they had not returned. Data supplied by Uttamchandani enabled the development of a focused campaign that yielded a short-term incremental revenue gain of $1 million from these so-called "lapsed" guests for an investment of just $30,000.

To support another marketing program, Uttamchandani modeled existing Most Valued Guests (MVGs) based on recency and frequency of stays, and revenue. She then mined the database to find guests with similar profiles, on the assumption that with targeted marketing and communications, they too could become MVGs. Programs designed for a group of guests fitting the profile yielded 30 percent more revenue than was generated from a control group of guests with a similar profile that received no special marketing. The program also earned Affinia Hospitality a gold medal award in the multichannel marketing category from the National Center for Database Marketing at its conference in 2005.

Along the way, as demand for data and new reports had grown, Uttamchandani had added one and then a second person to her team. As requests for more reports grew, the team began to apply a filter to help set priorities. Requests that had the potential to drive revenue, manage costs, or guide strategic direction received the highest priority.

The BI team also moved reporting online, creating an executive dashboard with in-depth drilldown capabilities. Internally branded The Pulse, the daily dashboard gathered together reports on key performance indicators for the entire business as well as each hotel property on a daily basis. For the first time, Affinia Hospitality top management—including the general managers of individual hotel properties—had daily access to a wide range of performance data and could compare the performance of each hotel with others in the Affinia family.

Not only did The Pulse help focus top management on its key performance indicators, but it also gave the general managers of each hotel greater visibility into their own performance compared with their peers, which allowed them to take more responsibility for the performance of the specific property under their management and to share best practices.

Before long, DHG also began to regard The Pulse and its underlying data as an advantage when competing for guests and staff with operators of comparable hotels and—when in conversations with hotels for management contracts—a unique selling point.

An Ownership Change Spawns a Brand-New Company

Of all the changes Affinia Hospitality went through between 2000 and 2005, none had changed the company as dramatically as what was to come next. In early 2006, Brooke Barrett and Patrick Denihan—two of Benjamin Denihan's children and two of the six equal partners who owned and managed the company after his death—bought out the other four partners through a half-billion-dollar recapitalization and became owners and co-CEOs of a new company now known as Denihan Hospitality Group.

Barrett and Denihan literally grew up in the family business, both having worked in it during summer and vacation breaks from school. Barrett was 26 and Denihan 20 when they joined the family business full time, and both have worked in the company continuously for the past 30-plus years.

According to Barrett, the decision she and her brother made to buy out the other four family partners was not based on

disagreements over the company's growth and expansion strategy or because they could not work together. Says Barrett:
"Some people just thought it was time to sell and Patrick and I
thought it was time to buy."

After taking control of the company, Barrett and Denihan immediately began to accelerate its national expansion
plans. Within weeks, DHG bought its first hotel outside of New
York—the Fitzpatrick Chicago—and rebranded it the Affinia
Chicago. In 2007, DHG expanded to Washington, D.C., with
a management contract for an independent hotel there.

In early 2008, the company acquired The James Hotel Group
and brand, and its single property, The James Chicago hotel.
DHG spent $119 million to acquire the 300-room hotel and,
later in the year, spent another $65 million to buy out its majority
partner in the 132-suite Surrey Hotel on New York's Upper East
Side, which it closed for an extensive remodeling. Known as a
branding, marketing, and customer service innovator, DHG also
was recognized as one of the Top 100 Management Companies
in 2008 by *Hotel Business Magazine*.[2]

In early 2009, DHG was awarded the management contract
for the Buckingham, an independent hotel on West 57th Street
and Sixth Avenue in Manhattan.

Today, Barrett oversees long-term strategic hotel operations,
sales and marketing, revenue management, human resources,
and information technology for DHG's entire portfolio of hotels
as well as independent affiliate hotels managed by DHG.
Denihan directs DHG's investments, finance, and growth strategies. Together they share responsibility for the vision, business
strategy, and growth of the company through acquisitions,
partnerships, and management contracts. Still family-owned

---

[2]Staff Report, "Top 100 Management Companies," *Hotel Business Magazine* (April 7, 2008).

and privately held, DHG has annual revenues of about $250 million.

The Economy Puts the Brakes on Rapid Growth

Three years in, the buyout seems to have created opportunity and challenge in equal measure. DHG now has the flexibility of three award-winning brands—each one targeting affluent travelers but with different demographic and psychographic characteristics—12 boutique and luxury hotels owned or under management in New York, Chicago, and Washington, D.C., and a reported $50 million in ready equity. In a different economy, by all measures DHG would be poised for explosive growth. However, with credit markets frozen, growth through acquisition will have to wait. In the meantime, according to Barrett, DHG is emphasizing management contracts over acquisitions.

Barrett and Denihan also find themselves managing a kind of revolution of culture as they work to build a cohesive management team of individuals with dramatically different backgrounds, experiences, and perspectives on the company. Some key managers have been with the company for decades—dating back to when Benjamin Denihan was the owner-operator. Others joined the company between 1999 and 2005, when it was beginning to accelerate its growth but before the recapitalization. Still others were brought in since 2006 specifically to help the company execute the most aggressive expansion plan in its history.

Says Barrett, "Our culture evolves every day. We have people who have been with us for a long time and are very good. And we have new people with different talents and that has raised the bar. As an owner, that's very exciting, but we do have the challenges of old and new. A lot of the creative tension exists around where we are with both talent and the use of information."

The Seeds of a Data-Driven Culture Are Planted

One of DHG's long-time executives is John Moser, the company's Chief Brand and Marketing Officer. Moser has been with the company for 25 years and became its CMO in 2003. In that year alone, he was responsible for rebranding MESH into Affinia Hospitality, launching the Affinia hotels brand, and opening the first Affinia-branded hotel. Moser oversees marketing, advertising, public relations, and web strategy for DHG, Affinia hotels, The Benjamin, and The James. He drove the creation of The Benjamin brand and was general manager of The Benjamin hotel while it was being built in 1998 and when it opened in 1999. Moser was named one of the "Top 25 Minds in Sales and Marketing for 2008" by the Hospitality Sales and Marketing Association International.

Moser is one of the company's biggest champions of its BI initiative—not surprisingly as the effort originally was focused on supporting marketing and sales. "Whether we're repositioning a property or developing a new marketing program, I'm the first one who wants more data to make sure we're hitting the target," says Moser.

Moser's commitment to data dates back to 1998 when he was creating The Benjamin brand. He was given a "blank canvas" and the charter to build a luxury property on the same block as one of the company's three-star hotels but with one caveat: The Benjamin could not take business from the existing hotel, but it certainly could take business from the Waldorf-Astoria located right across the street. Moser decided that extensive research that would allow him to identify a customer that he could precisely target with the new brand would be essential to achieving this objective.

At the time, the company did not have a way to efficiently mine the guest data it had been collecting since 1997, and so Moser had to use more informal methods of researching potential target customers, including the use of an advisory board comprising his contacts in the field. He ultimately decided that The Benjamin would differentiate itself by catering to the luxury business traveler. "Lots of hotels do this now, but The Benjamin was one of the first to include a full-size desk and ergonomic chair, and a printer/scanner/copier and high-speed Internet access in every room that was easy to use," says Moser.

He credits that decision with The Benjamin's success at attracting a new type of customer without cannibalizing its sister property down the street. The experience also cemented his own belief in the importance of data in decision making, says Moser.

The experience contributed as well to Barrett and Cahill's interest in funding a BI initiative. And, it marked the beginning of the company's transition to a data-driven organization, which is a prerequisite to achieving the transparency and accountability that are the hallmark of a performance-directed culture.

Moser views DHG's efforts to become a performance-directed culture as a work in progress. "We have great transparency," he says, "but I don't think we always use it as effectively as we could. Everyone is interested in some of the things that are really easy to understand, like how a hotel is performing, what the cost per occupied room is, and so on. But fewer people are interested in some of the more exotic data we use to make marketing decisions—things like guest preferences and behavior and other information that isn't as clear-cut."

"It's funny because whenever I say we need to do some surveying or gather some data, some of our executives still say to me, 'Do we have to do that? Can't we just use what we already have?' And I say that our use of information is what differentiates us because everybody else is just kind of doing it by the seat of their pants."

New Talent Brings Different Perspectives

Between 1999 and 2005, as DHG gradually began to add outsiders to its management ranks, most new hires seem to have been recruited as much for their cultural fit as for their ability to bring industry experience and functional expertise. CIO Cahill was one such hire, and BI expert Uttamchandani was another.

A hire that ventured into bolder territory occurred in 2005 when DHG added Beverly Ramsook as its Vice President of Revenue Management. Revenue management is a discipline that applies a combination of complex formulas and gut feel based on experience to get the right price from the right customer for a perishable product or service. Perishable in this context means services such as a hotel room—if a hotel room stands empty for a night, there is no chance to recover the lost revenue. Revenue management explains why a person who made a hotel reservation months in advance can pay one price for a room and another person who made a reservation today can pay another price entirely.

Ramsook is highly regarded inside DHG, and recruiting her was considered a coup. At the time of her hire, Ramsook was working in New York City at AccorHotels, the third largest hotel company in the world at the time, and she previously had worked for the Palace Hotel in New York. According to her peers at DHG, Ramsook brought a new level of professionalism and aggressiveness to revenue management at the company and has been an avid user and champion of BI. "Revenue managers live and die on data," says Ramsook. "And even though I worked for a very large hotel company that had BI, I was very impressed by what I saw at DHG when I came here. And it has only gotten better in the last four years."

However, Ramsook acknowledges that not all the revenue managers working at DHG when she joined the company were

users of the BI reports. "A lot of the people in revenue management positions in the company grew up here," she says.
"Because BI was still new to the company, it was new to them
and many of them were uncomfortable using it."

According to Ramsook, some of the revenue managers
were open to being coached and others weren't. The ones
who weren't ultimately were asked to leave the company and
replaced by people for whom making revenue management
decisions based on data was second nature.

A similar newer hire is Tom Felderman, who came to DHG
in 2006 from Fairmont Resorts and Hotels as Vice President of
Finance. Felderman's charter was to modernize DHG's financial
statements and reporting. "It was a very interesting time," he
says. "Brooke and Patrick had just recapitalized the company,
changed the name of the company, and really were essentially
starting over. I came in right after that happened and the mes-
sage was, 'We're a new company; we're a different company; we
need to change; we need to grow.' So I took that and ran with
it, and from a financial standpoint turned the company upside
down in that first year."

According to Felderman, two of the people who had to
change first were Brooke Barrett and Patrick Denihan. For example, Denihan had a practice of reading every financial statement
cover-to-cover, line-by-line, every month, and then going to
every hotel's monthly review meeting and talking to the general
managers about their revenue and expenses in detail. Moreover,
because the business was a closely held, family-owned company, the financial statements were designed to be meaningful
only to insiders.

Says Felderman: "I'm sure there was a time when that
level of scrutiny from Patrick was important. But this was 2006
and the company wanted to grow and expand, and needed
to attract investors to finance it." Felderman believed that if
DHG was to be successful, the co-CEOs needed to focus

on more strategic issues and the company needed financial statements that would satisfy sophisticated outside institutional investors.

According to Felderman, as the new financial statements took shape and people in the company became more comfortable with them, Denihan refocused his attention on bigger picture issues. Some of the people who worked for Felderman in the finance department, however, were not quite so flexible or focused on future success.

When Felderman came to DHG, the company's financial processes were outdated, some were manual, and some members of the finance staff were long-time company employees who had not necessarily been trained in finance. As a result, it routinely took up to six weeks to close the books and produce financial statements. It was clear to Felderman right away that he needed to overhaul just about everything that was going on in finance, and some people were not very happy about it. As Felderman says: "Imagine a company that's been privately owned forever and imagine that you have worked with the company for your entire career. A new person comes in and says, 'We're going to do things differently.' How do you think you would react?"

Felderman's approach to managing change was to get people to see that there were other ways to do things, better ways to do things. "It wasn't about changing things just to change things or to make it difficult for people so they will leave," he says. "It was about productivity, about spending an hour less on some trivial task so people could spend an hour more on something that's more beneficial to the company."

However, during this time of change in the finance department, some employees were just not able to get on board and were asked to leave the company—still a relatively rare occurrence within DHG that added to a sense that things at DHG were changing.

Operational and Financial Data Come Together

With the basic overhaul of financial systems at DHG completed, finance became the next focus of the company's BI initiative—an effort that was mostly complete as of this writing in early 2009. With that, DHG top management now has integrated access to both operational and financial data in the same report—The Pulse—a capability that also was rolled out to general managers in late 2008. Operational data is available daily and financial data is available once a month when the books close.

So does this mean that the general managers of the hotel properties are now being held accountable to meet performance expectations that are reported on in The Pulse? Apparently, the answer is a qualified "yes." The general managers have access to detailed information about the performance of their hotels and have the authority to make all decisions that would improve their key performance indicators. What they do not have is the authority to deviate from brand standards and centralized corporate policies.

This is quite a change for DHG. When Felderman joined the company, for example, many functions for the hotels that in most companies would be the domain of the general manager were driven out of shared services. The costs for them would end up on the profit and loss statements of each hotel as four or five line items labeled "corporate allocation." This meant that not only could the general managers not control those expenses, but they often did not know what they were.

Felderman worked to get the hotel profit and loss statements to look more like those of a typical hotel, and as that occurred, general managers could see the details of what they were paying for. This created more transparency, but did not solve the accountability piece. How could general managers be held accountable for expenses they had no control over?

More recently, though, the company has begun to push some of its shared services out to the hotel properties and now they work much more in concert with the general managers. Andy Labetti, general manager of The Benjamin hotel, confirms that shift. Labetti is a returning DHG employee, having worked as assistant general manager of The Benjamin. He left the company in 2003 to work for Four Seasons, but returned in August 2007.

Labetti says that a lot has changed in the nearly five years he was away from the company. "From my perspective, today I feel that the results for my hotel rest on my shoulders. I have a lot of help—people I can go to for advice. But people support me; they don't tell me what to do. I think all our general managers are increasingly running the show and we're getting better at it."

The MESH that Labetti left was a much more centralized company than DHG, he says. Sales and revenue management is much more coordinated presently with the general managers, for one thing. For another, he says he knows much more now what is expected of him than he did his first time around at the company. And, he is a heavy user of The Pulse.

"The Pulse is invaluable," says Labetti. "It gives me somewhat of a crystal ball and helps me make sound decisions. We are beating the competition right now, even in this economy, and with The Pulse, I sometimes feel like I have the answers to the test before the test."

Co-CEO Barrett says of DHG's move to a more distributed services model, "It is certainly a work in progress.... We don't think the centralized structure is necessarily right, especially outside of New York City. We are exploring a hybrid model of centralized services in different locations depending on the situation. We've been treading lightly in Chicago, for example."

Widening Cultural Divide?

Despite the clear progress DHG has made on the path to becoming a performance-directed culture, the company has a ways to go. Three new hires in 2008 together represent DHG's biggest departure from the past, and while the three have superb track records of success in the hotel industry, their arrival also has brought the cultural differences between what Barrett calls "the old and the new" into sharper focus.

With the acquisition of The James Hotel Group in early 2008, DHG also "acquired" Brad Wilson, who is now DHG's Chief Operating Officer, and Danette Opaczewski, Senior Vice President of Asset Management. Wilson was CEO of The James Hotel Group at the time of its acquisition by DHG and Opaczewski was its Chief Financial Officer. Prior to that, Wilson was Vice President of Operations for W Hotels and a key member of its founding team, and in his 20-year career worked his way up through the ranks at several hotel chains. Before joining The James Hotel Group, Opaczewski was general manager of the Royalton, a luxury hotel in New York City.

It's worth noting that The James, W Hotels, and the Royalton are all successful hotel brands that stand in sharp contrast to the comfort and convenience of the Affinia brand and the understated traditional luxury of The Benjamin brand. The adjectives often applied to them are "stylish," "sleek," and "hip." The differences between these new DHG brands and the existing DHG brands provide some insight into the differences in perspectives and management styles that are now coming together in the company.

In August 2008, Pam Suhr joined DHG as Senior Vice President of Operations, responsible for the day-to-day operations of DHG's portfolio of 12 hotels across three brands. Suhr previously had worked in top management positions for Crescent Hotels and Resorts, HEI Resorts and Hotels, and Interstate Hotels and Resorts where over a 14-year period she helped take the once-privately held company from 23 properties to 400 through a series of mergers and an initial public offering.

More than other key managers hired at DHG in the past decade, Wilson, Opaczewski, and Suhr bring different viewpoints to the company. They all came from very senior positions in very successful companies focused on aggressive growth. The positions they now hold are essential to DHG's success going forward—evidence that their hiring likely signals a desire on the part of Barrett and Denihan to move the company into a higher gear. And, with their differences in backgrounds and experience come inevitable differences of opinion about how things should work.

For example, when Wilson talks about DHG, he says, "Data is essential to get to the core truth, and to encourage thinking and decision making at every level in the company. So the question is, how do you get people to start thinking at every level? You get them to collaborate and cross-communicate and all that good stuff. So that's what we're trying to do."

Another source of frustration for Wilson is what he calls the company's lack of conflict resolution processes. "I always hear that consensus is very important at DHG," he says. "And then you talk to eight people who were in the same meeting where there was a consensus, and it turns out it's a false consensus. The more we work from the same scorecard, the more we can achieve true consensus."

Wilson also says, "Focusing more on quantifiable results through the consistent use of data creates a different kind of tension than this company is used to."

Another point of difference between what some in the company call the old guard versus the new is around DHG's efforts to achieve more transparency and accountability. Of these efforts, Pam Suhr says: "I don't think transparency is here yet at this company and accountability is just underway. We are just at the early stages of it. And this just is as a point of comparison to what I've experienced before."

In addition, she says, while DHG has the tools in place to use data to support theories and drive decisions with The Pulse report, its usage is not yet widespread within operations. And, with multiple constituencies to support, The Pulse reports on a wide range of metrics, and Suhr believes that the company's approach of providing detailed reports on multiple performance metrics to everyone is premature. All of the general managers of DHG properties report to Suhr, who is responsible for day-to-day hotel operations, and her preference would be "to have general managers focus on a couple of key pieces, and really get it and understand those pieces before looking at everything."

Opaczewski agrees. "I came from a company that did not have extensive data management, but what we had was very specific to our accountability versus trying to look at everything. So, when I first came here and met with Menka and went through the BI tools, I thought it was brilliant in that it was so detailed that it could really be utilized to grow the company in a very competitive way. But there was so much of it and to find what you were looking for has been a struggle."

To address these concerns, the BI team plans to create a set of high-level management reports for the general managers and others who do not need the in-depth information that functional experts need on a daily basis. They will still be able to use the detailed reporting when they need to.

These differences in perspective aside, Wilson gives Barrett and Denihan credit for the bold step they took in bringing in people with styles that "are the antithesis of their company." What is common, according to Wilson, are shared values.

"It's a very interesting fit," says Wilson. "The James was a small entrepreneurial hotel, creative, low structure, not bureaucratic, instinct-oriented. DHG was a collection of 12 hotels that were heavily structured, process and directive-driven, bureaucratic. But there was a shared value in both companies about how you treat people, considering them, caring about them in the decision-making process. I think caring is a big shared value. So even though we have different approaches, I think they saw that at the core, we are the same."

Bringing Everything Together

Brooke Barrett understands clearly the challenge she and her brother face in bringing together such a diverse group of people to take DHG to the next level. "It's a challenge in any company," she says. "You must get everything out on the table and acknowledge it, but with respect for everyone's background."

"Since we recapitalized the company, though, we have a lot at stake," says Barrett. "We can't wait, we must make fast decisions and we must hold people accountable. But we also have to be clear about what we hold near and dear . . . what we don't want to give up."

And, according to Barrett, DHG's culture of caring is one of the values the company will never give up.

DHG and the Performance Culture Maturity Model

With a clear understanding of where DHG started in its quest to become a performance-directed culture and where it is today, it's instructive to gauge its progress using my Performance Culture Maturity Model (see Figure 2.1).

(Continued)

FIGURE 2.1 Denihan Hospitality Group and the Performance Culture Maturity Model™

	Alignment with Mission	Transparency and Accountability	Action on Insights	Conflict Resolution	Common Trust in Data	Availability and Currency of Information
Performance-Directed Culture Realized	Actionable and embraced mission—supported, informed, and reinforced by metrics [2009]	General transparency and accountability accepted as cultural tenets	"Closed loop" processes ensure timely, concerted action	Established and effective mechanisms for resolving conflicts	Data as truth: Common application of data, filters, rules, and semantics [2007]	Currency of metrics/data matches rhythm of business [2009]
Performance-Directed Culture Emerging	Actionable mission supported by "top-down" metrics [2006]	Limited transparency and accountability; multiple functions collaborate [2009]	Ad hoc (informal) action on insights across functions [2009]	When identified, conflicts resolved on an impromptu basis [2009]	Common data: Provincial views and semantics used to support specific positions [2009]	Enterprise availability, uneven currency of information [2007] [2008]
Departmental Optimization	Alignment with discrete functional goals, not enterprise mission [2001]	Fragmented transparency and accountability within discrete functions [2001]	Uncoordinated/ parochial action (sometimes at the expense of others) [2002]	Appearance of cooperation, "opportunistic reconciliation" [2007]	Conflicting, functional views of data cause confusion, disagreement [2002] [2008] [2001]	Availability and currency directed by departmental sources [2001]
Chaos Reigns	Mission not actionable, not communicated, and/or not understood [2000]	Arbitrary accountability, general opacity [2000]	Insights rarely leveraged [2000]	Conflicting, redundant, and competing efforts are the norm [2000]	Data and information generally unreliable and distrusted [2001] [2000] [2000]	Multiple, inconsistent data sources, conflicting semantics [2001] [2000] [2000]

Source: © 2009 Patent Pending Dresner Advisory Services, LLC

The first phase of DHG's journey occurred in 2000 and 2001, when Barrett and Cahill decided to recruit a BI expert to assist with a BI initiative. The second phase began with the 9/11 attacks in New York and continued through DHG's recovery and for the next several years thereafter. The third phase unfolded in 2005 and 2006, when Barrett and Denihan recapitalized the company to buy out the other four partners. The fourth phase took place over 2006 and 2008 with several strategic acquisitions, an infusion of new management, and the introduction of new policies and procedures. The fifth phase started in late 2008 and will likely continue as long as the recession does, unless an internal or external event dramatically changes the company's course.

We can safely assume that when DHG was MESH, the company would have scored at the bottom in practically all categories of the Maturity Model. It was a tactically driven organization that lacked a clear vision and strategy due to fragmented and nonaligned ownership. Each of the six equal partners drove initiatives based on their own interests and views of the business. For example, it was common among key managers, when seeking approval for a project, to approach a partner known to favor it and obtain that partner's permission. Consensus was not always necessary.

Access to most performance information related to the business was restricted to use by the partners. The organization was as opaque as possible, with employees given directives, not goals, objectives, or metrics. No significant debate or discussions about direction, strategy, or tactics occurred beyond the six partners. As a result, employees could not be held fully accountable if an initiative failed, since they merely were following orders or carrying out assigned tasks and had no direct control over the decision.

(Continued)

This sort of environment and culture do not usually generate much conflict. However, when conflict did arise, it generally was not resolved definitively.

And finally, even though data was being collected in operational systems, it generally was not used to support better performance management capabilities. Hence for both Common Trust in Data and Availability and Currency of Information, DHG would have scored at the bottom since BI programs had not yet been initiated.

Phase I: 2000–2001

As previously mentioned, when Barrett and Cahill decided to hire a BI expert to help them start harvesting data, they could not have known that 9/11 was just around the corner and how important access to data would become in its aftermath. Barrett put it this way: "I think the whole strategy of using all of your data as an enabler to help you make decisions is a mind-set that has grown and changed over time. When people who have recently joined us discover what I like to call the 'competitive advantage' with our approach to Business Intelligence—especially for the size of our company—they're really blown away. And the more they understand it, the more there is a demand for using it to enable better decision making."

With this decision and with 9/11, DHG started down the path to becoming a data-driven company. As a result, although other criteria remained roughly the same, the two technology category criteria began to rise and transparency also began to improve.

Initial reaction among key stakeholders was positive. According to DHG's Chief Brand and Marketing Officer, John Moser, "When this new resource first came in to the company I was really excited about what it could bring to me in sales and marketing," and "what good information we could have about who our customer was. I've always been very focused on trying to understand our customer and allow the customer to have a bigger say in what our products should be and what our services should be, how we should move forward. Before we had Menka, we really didn't have the ability to understand our customers as well as we do now."

Like never before, DHG now had (limited) fact-based systems with which to determine performance and drive limited changes in order to optimize marketing programs. According to Moser, previously it sometimes had been difficult to lobby for additional programs without hard data to substantiate opportunities. "Now I actually have to say not only is it my idea but here's what the customer said," he says.

As a result, in Phase I, I estimate that DHG climbed into the Departmental Optimization category for Transparency and Accountability, Common Trust in Data, and Availability and Currency of Information on my Maturity Model—a significant improvement in such a short time.

Phase II: 9/11 and Beyond

DHG's successful recovery after 9/11, and the role BI played in it, created real urgency across the organization to leverage information in the BI system as a means of not just survival but competitive advantage. The period immediately following 9/11 solidified the company's commitment to BI and performance management, and facilitated DHG's achievement of a data-driven culture—a key milestone on the way toward a performance-directed culture. As a result of this response to 9/11 with BI, by 2002, DHG managed to elevate its Action on Insights and Common Trust in Data scores up one level.

(Continued)

Phase III: 2005–2006

During this period DHG recapitalized and consolidated management from six down to two more-visionary owners, with a strategy for growth. At this point, the company had begun to reinvent itself and BI was elevated to "strategic." A clearer mission statement and strategy had become evident—with a focus upon growth and the intent to become a more prominent and national collection of hotels. The new strategy was explained to me in this way: "We want to be the best operator of upscale luxury hotels in the United States and, as evidence of that, we want to grow the company. We don't want to be 12 hotels, we want to be 20 or 30 hotels and we want to see that success recognized by our customers, our employees, and our investors".

With a more clearly articulated, communicated, and actionable mission and a clear strategy, DHG's score for Alignment with Mission climbs to Performance-Directed Culture Emerging.

Phase IV: 2006–2008

While DHG was acquiring a new property and a management contract outside of New York City and bringing new management into areas such as revenue management, finance, and hotel operations, the company also was expanding its BI initiatives. Under the direction of Beverly Ramsook, DHG's new Vice President of Revenue Management, that function especially embraced BI. As Ramsook says: "Obviously we were better, we were faster at making our decisions; we made pressure decisions."

Ramsook also shared an anecdote that illustrates the power of DHG's use of fact-based decision making and the data-driven culture that had emerged. Early in Ramsook's tenure at the company, there was a time when many hotels in the city were offering special promotions for Sunday nights. For many hotels, Sunday is the worst night, with leisure travelers returning home from the weekend and business travelers planning Monday arrivals. The typical offer, according to Ramsook, was $50 off for a Sunday night stay.

Says Ramsook: "Our marketing team wanted to make the same kind of Sunday night offer. So I said, 'Hey, could you let me see the data on how we do against the competitive sets on Sunday nights?' As it turned out we actually did extremely well on Sundays—it was our best night. So there was no reason for us to give away $50."

Instances like this helped elevate DHG's position for both Common Trust in Data and Availability and Currency of Information on the Maturity Model. At this point, the company was making great strides toward a performance-directed culture.

Also during this time, a new set of organizational dynamics began to emerge as new management began to change some key business processes and roles and responsibilities to better align operations with DHG's mission. For example, starting in 2006, hotel general managers were expected to take greater responsibility for the performance of their respective properties.

According to DHG COO Brad Wilson, this was a natural shift because the company was moving from being very focused on a small cluster of New York City hotels to adding properties outside of New York and also to managing hotels for other owners. "We had to move from a company with general managers basically just checking people in and out and making sure they were happy ... to really running the business day to day."

This transition caused some tension in the organization, including in BI where different applications in newly

(Continued)

acquired properties were not yet integrated into the model, which caused DHG to regress on some attributes on the Maturity Model. However, related changes drove positive progress on other fronts. For example, added transparency in the sales call center had a tremendous impact when people started using the new applications. Says Wilson: "All of a sudden people knew how many calls every reservation agent makes every day. Everybody knows how much revenue each agent books every day. We add on top of it a sales-focused approach where people are thinking about how much additional up-sell money each agent brings in every day."

In addition, as never before, conflicts were beginning to be aired more openly, with divergent views being heard and considered. As a result, DHG climbed by a full level in Conflict Resolution during this period.

According to DHG CIO John Cahill: "We're learning to not be so nice to each other and to challenge and to ask questions and to probe more deeply. That is filtering down through the organization and because the data is available to answer those questions, it's not a 'gotcha' kind of a thing. It's, 'Hey, you should be looking at this because you will be smarter about how to do things tomorrow than you were yesterday.' And that's all part of the continuous learning process that we try to foster and engender inside the organization."

Phase V: Late 2008 and Beyond

In mid-2008, it became clear that the United States was in the midst of a significant economic recession. As a result, DHG had to alter its strategy for aggressive growth, with many programs aimed at supporting growth—including BI—being postponed or trimmed. However, during this period, DHG was able to complete a finance BI project that integrated operational and financial information on The Pulse report, which had a very positive impact upon Availability and Currency of Information, Common Trust in Data and resulted in increased Transparency and Accountability.

By all measures, the progress that DHG has made toward a performance-directed culture is extraordinary. DHG demonstrates a pattern similar to other successful companies that I've evaluated: An internal or external event serves as a wake-up call for management—for DHG, this was 9/11—which elevates the importance of BI and performance management. Shortly thereafter, a data-driven culture emerges. With a data-driven culture in place, transparency and accountability can follow, allowing the company to make significant progress towards a performance-directed culture.

CHAPTER 3

Cleveland Clinic

It would be hard to find a more performance-directed health-care provider than Cleveland Clinic—at least when it comes to medical innovation, patient outcomes, and cutting-edge health-care delivery.

Cleveland Clinic is one of the largest and, by most measures, one of the best healthcare providers in the world. According to the most respected annual survey of hospitals in the United States,[1] Cleveland Clinic consistently ranks among the top four. For 14 years in a row, it has been ranked #1 in heart care. In 10 of the 16 specialties evaluated by the survey, Cleveland Clinic ranks in the top 10.

A not-for-profit multispecialty academic medical center that integrates clinical and hospital care with research and education, Cleveland Clinic was founded in 1921 and is headquartered in Cleveland, Ohio. In addition to its 1,400-bed main campus, it has an integrated staff model and hospital in Florida; eight community hospitals; a children's hospital for rehabilitation; two affiliate hospitals; numerous family health centers offering outpatient, primary, and home healthcare; and facilities in Canada, Nevada, and Abu Dhabi.

---

[1]Staff Report, "America's Best Hospitals," *U.S. News & World Report*, July 2008.

In 2008, Cleveland Clinic had 2,000 salaried physicians and scientists on staff representing 120 specialties and subspecialties, and a total of 40,000 employees in the system. It recorded 3.3 million total visits and more than 165,000 system admissions. Its operating revenue reached $4.8 billion in fiscal year 2007, and its operating income was just shy of $350 million.[2]

Because of its stellar reputation, patients come to Cleveland Clinic from all across America and more than 80 nations, including many famous patients, from businesspeople and politicians to entertainers and heads of state. Over the years, notable patients have included William Randolph Hearst,[3] King Hussein of Jordan,[4] Liza Minnelli,[5] Bob Dole,[6] and Robin Williams.[7]

Determined to Lead

Not surprisingly, Cleveland Clinic is known for its long list of "medical firsts," including the first coronary angiography performed by Dr. Mason Sones in 1958, the first coronary bypass surgery by Dr. Rene Favaloro in 1967, and the first U.S. face transplant by Dr. Maria Siemionow in December 2008.

When the face transplant recipient—46-year-old mother of two, Connie Culp—held a press conference in May 2009 revealing for the first time the results of her 22-hour surgery, the world was transfixed. The victim of a shotgun blast that nearly

---

[2]Financial results for FY2008 had not been reported as of this writing.
[3]"Press: Forest City Fusion," *TIME*, October 10, 1932.
[4]"King Hussein in Cleveland," *New York Times*, February 4, 1984.
[5]"Liza Minnelli Hospitalized with Encephalitis," *CNN.com*, October 23, 2000.
[6]"Bob Dole to Undergo Surgery to Correct Enlarged Aorta," *CNN.com*, June 26, 2001.
[7]"Robin Williams Recovering from Heart Surgery," *TMZ*, March 23, 2009.

obliterated her face five years ago, Culp now can breathe without a tracheotomy tube in her throat, can eat solid foods, and has regained her sense of smell.[8] The combination of regaining the basic functions most people take for granted and her near-normal appearance is a powerful reminder of how Cleveland Clinic is advancing transplant medicine through groundbreaking surgical procedures.

Cleveland Clinic has been at the forefront of advances in other aspects of medicine as well. A long-time advocate of keeping patients informed about the quality of their care, in 1998 the Clinic began publishing detailed information and data for healthcare providers about its treatments, including summaries of surgical and medical trends, data on patient volume and outcomes, and reviews of new technologies and innovations at Cleveland Clinic. It now publishes annually 27 different Outcomes Books on a wide range of diseases and conditions, and increases the number each year.

Largely because of Cleveland Clinic, other leading U.S. healthcare providers have adopted the practice of making patient outcomes public. This greater transparency around how medicine is practiced and its efficacy is a welcome trend in a field that traditionally has resisted detailed public scrutiny about its performance.

Cleveland Clinic also is a pioneer in the use of the Internet in medical applications, offering a broad range of services, including online second opinions, which allow patients and their healthcare providers to consult with Clinic physicians on treatment options and alternatives. In May 2009, the Clinic created accounts on Facebook, Twitter, and LinkedIn that it will use together with a YouTube channel it had created earlier in the

---

[8]Madison Park, "First U.S. Face Transplant Recipient Offers Thanks," *CNN.com*, May 5, 2009.

year to deliver health information and news to a larger community, interact with patients, and provide a social community for employees.

Among a still-small minority of institutions in the country to digitize patients' medical records, in February 2008, Cleveland Clinic announced a pilot program with Google to test secure exchange of data between its electronic records and a Google profile in clinical settings. The ultimate aim is to put patients in charge of their medical records and improve the efficiency of interactions between multiple physicians, healthcare providers, and pharmacies.

Cleveland Clinic is bold in other ways as well, for example, by stepping out front in addressing one of medicine's most sensitive controversies right now: potential conflicts of interest arising from financial relationships between physicians, and pharmaceutical and other medical companies. In December 2008, the Clinic began publicly disclosing all of the business relationships between its staff doctors and scientists, and drug and device makers—the first major healthcare provider in the country to do so. The action is part of a larger initiative that includes more stringent conflict-of-interest policies, a formal tracking and reporting system, and a committee that formally reviews any significant relationships.

Less dramatic—but no less important—Cleveland Clinic also is credited with breaking new ground by adopting more effective ways of organizing to deliver medical care. In March 2009, the Clinic was honored by the American Medical Group Association for its accomplishments in managing the medical group model of care, which is based on multispecialty groups of physicians rather than solo practices.

The award recognized Cleveland Clinic specifically for having completely reorganized its clinical services over the prior two years, dissolving siloed functional divisions such as medicine and surgery, and replacing them with practice units based around specific diseases, organ systems, and common clinical needs. The practice units—there are 26 of them and Cleveland Clinic calls them Institutes—are designed to improve the patient experience through collaboration while eliminating internal competition and redundancy.

While its recent reorganization takes the medical group model to another level, Cleveland Clinic was actually an early adopter of the model, its founders having used it as an organizing principle from the very beginning. When Drs. George Crile, Frank Bunts, William Lower, and Stephen Phillips formed Cleveland Clinic 88 years ago, only the Mayo Clinic in Rochester, Minnesota, and military units practiced medicine this way. All four physicians had served in the military in combat situations in various wars, and had come away from their experiences energized by the possibilities of applying this particular military medical practice to civilian medical care.

As common as the medical group model is today, when Cleveland Clinic was founded, it was considered a radical idea. Until the late 1800s, medical care in America was delivered in direct relationships between individual physicians and their patients. When the first medical groups were formed, sole practitioners feared them because of the implication that they could provide better and more comprehensive care. At the very least, medical groups were a threat because they could provide more consistent availability of medical care on nights, weekends, and holidays. Some felt that medical groups violated the sanctity of the doctor–patient relationship by placing an organization between physicians and their patients. It took many years for the medical community to fully embrace the medical group model—which it did in large part because institutions like the Mayo Clinic and Cleveland Clinic led the way.

The Gap between Medical Excellence and Business Performance

Given its performance orientation in the practice of medicine and delivery of medical care, you might expect Cleveland Clinic to have an equally impressive track record of innovation in managing the financial, operational, and administrative aspects of the institution. In this arena, though, Cleveland Clinic's progress over the decades has been slow and uneven. It's fair to ask why.

One reason is that the traditional approach to healthcare management has been to separate treatment from administration, putting clinicians in charge of medical affairs and business-people in charge of the business. And, even though Cleveland Clinic more often than not has appointed clinicians to its top executive spot—five out of the six chief executives in its history have been physicians—the Clinic often has struggled with the inherent tension between medical management and business management. There have been crucial times in its history when these tensions caused serious conflicts. One of those times was the decade following the retirement in 1940 of Cleveland Clinic's first president, one of its four founders, Dr. George Crile.

Crile was a brilliant surgeon and a dynamic, strong-willed individual who was widely acknowledged as the driving force behind Cleveland Clinic in its early years. While the other three founders shared his views, it was his proposal to form Cleveland Clinic as a group of physicians who would "act as a unit."[9]

---

[9]Some of the details of the history of Cleveland Clinic are based on two books: John D. Clough, *To Act as a Unit: The Story of the Cleveland Clinic*. 4th ed. (Cleveland: Cleveland Clinic Press, 2004); and John A. Kastor, MD, *Specialty Care in the Era of Managed Care: Cleveland Clinic Versus University Hospitals of Cleveland* (Baltimore: John Hopkins University Press, 2005).

It was also Crile's idea to establish Cleveland Clinic as a not-for-profit corporation so that its physicians would not have to worry about bringing in business to earn money. While this presumably would allow them to focus on doing what was best for patients at all times, it also meant that Cleveland Clinic had no shareholders and therefore no rightful leaders. So the founders created a Board of Trustees and granted it the authority to appoint the Clinic's leaders. The first Trustees were the four founders and an attorney who handled Cleveland Clinic's legal needs; they quickly agreed to appoint Crile president.

In those early years, when Cleveland Clinic was small and its business operations relatively simple, this system of governance worked well. Adding to the Clinic's stability, all four founders were active and Crile provided exceptionally strong leadership. But dramatic events would soon alter the picture. One of the founders, Dr. Frank Bunts, died suddenly of a heart attack in 1928. Then in 1929, another founder, Dr. Stephen Phillips, died in a fire at Cleveland Clinic that claimed 123 lives, injured 50 people, and rendered the Clinic's main building unusable for a time. A few months later, the stock market crashed and the country was plunged into the Great Depression.

The two remaining founders, Crile and Dr. William Lower, were by then in their 60s, and they struggled under the weight of lawsuits and other financial obligations from the 1929 fire as well as the effects of a devastating economy. Even though Cleveland Clinic resumed its growth as soon as the economy began to rebound, it took until 1940 to meet all of its financial obligations and pay off all of its debts. By then in his 70s, Crile took the opportunity to retire. Astonishingly, despite Crile's age and failing health, Cleveland Clinic had done no succession planning and his departure created a leadership vacuum that would not be filled for many years.

Searching for Equilibrium

At the time Crile retired, the Board of Trustees was still the sole governing body of Cleveland Clinic—although it had expanded its membership—and was heavily involved in all aspects of the management of the Clinic. The Trustees took input from the group's staff physicians, but were not subject to their will. Without a strong leader, though, relationships among the more dominant personalities on the medical staff gradually deteriorated into conflicts and competitiveness. The relationship between the Trustees and the medical staff suffered as well.

Cleveland Clinic's governance system changed dramatically in 1955 when a Board of Governors made up of physicians—elected by other physicians in the group—was formed and over time assumed a larger role in the strategic and day-to-day management of the institution. From that point on, the Board of Trustees gradually ceded much of its authority to the Board of Governors, although the two Boards continued to work side by side on business issues.

Still, tension between the two Boards escalated because of differences of opinion over strategy, and especially over whether Cleveland Clinic should pursue an aggressive expansion plan. The Governors were in favor of it. Some of the Trustees, however, feared that the plan was imprudent and that the Governors lacked the business expertise to execute it successfully.

The conflict between the two Boards came to a head in 1968, and soon thereafter the Governors asserted control in what could be described as a bloodless coup. The Trustees turned their focus to a narrow set of fiscal issues and the Governors took on everything else. One of the most notable changes was that after a decade of businessmen in the top job at Cleveland Clinic, the Governors reinstated the practice of appointing clinicians to that post—a practice that continues to this day. After this transition was complete, the Board of Trustees' then-chairman declared, "Businessmen should stick to business issues and never get involved in medical affairs."[10]

The Times Are Changing

To put these events in perspective, the shift in the balance of power back to clinicians in the late 1960s predates much of the debate over healthcare reform that still rages in the United States. Today—with healthcare costs spiraling out of control and all of the key players either clamoring for or resigned to reform—it would be nearly impossible to make a strong case for the wisdom of a healthcare provider keeping its medical and business affairs separate.

Still, it's difficult to judge whether the events of 1968 impeded Cleveland Clinic's adoption of modern business management practices. What they certainly did, however, was cement the authority of Cleveland Clinic's medical staff, including with regards to any efforts to improve the business processes and performance of the Clinic. For example, while the medical superstars at Cleveland Clinic were encouraged—required, really—to demonstrate excellence in medicine, they were not always held to the same high standards when it came to the business. In fact, according to several long-time employees on the business side of the Clinic, top clinicians often were given a "free pass" when it came to conforming with practices, processes, and systems designed to improve business efficiency.

Moreover, it would take another 20 years for Cleveland Clinic to accept the need for strategic planning, strong financial and operational management, and marketing. And it took

---

[10]John A. Kastor, MD, *Specialty Care in the Era of Managed Care: Cleveland Clinic Versus University Hospitals of Cleveland* (Baltimore: John Hopkins University Press, 2005) p. 7.

even longer for the Clinic to launch formal business performance management initiatives that could be combined with its medical advances to produce better patient outcomes and patient satisfaction more efficiently and cost-effectively.

Time for Change

The seeds of Cleveland Clinic's first formal performance management initiatives can be found in the appointment of Dr. Floyd Loop as the Clinic's CEO in 1989. It was a time of financial turmoil and uncertainty for the Clinic. The rapid expansion that the Board of Trustees had feared back in the late 1960s had, in fact, taken its toll. For example, Cleveland Clinic's Florida facility was not yet self-supporting and it thrust the entire Clinic into the throes of a severe cash crunch.

In the tradition of physician-CEOs at Cleveland Clinic, Loop was a gifted surgeon. It was under his exacting leadership in the 1970s and 1980s that the Clinic rose to international prominence as a heart care center. As CEO, Loop quickly recognized that immediate and dramatic action was needed to return Cleveland Clinic to financial stability and get it back on track for growth.

After a short period in which he reorganized his management team to fill gaps and streamline reporting and decision making, Loop developed and executed a comprehensive economic recovery plan that included fixing inefficiencies in the way internal systems were managed and improving marketing to increase patient volume. The plan resulted in increased revenue and lower costs. By 1990, the cash flow problem had been solved and Cleveland Clinic resumed its growth plans, including those for geographic expansion.

Even though the acute financial crisis was over, Loop had the foresight to understand that Cleveland Clinic needed to put in place formal processes and systems for improving overall performance for the long haul. As a first step, in 1993, he initiated an effort to identify key operational drivers of financial performance so that they could be improved upon and people could be held accountable. Given the size of the Clinic and its geographically dispersed operations, having key performance indicators (KPIs) that everyone could understand was an essential component of a performance management system and essential in creating a culture of accountability, which was the effort's stated goal.

According to Tom Wadsworth, Senior Director, Medical Operations and Nursing at Cleveland Clinic, prior to this, the Clinic's performance metrics were based primarily on financial outcomes. By applying metrics to operational drivers, the Clinic could—among other things—align operational practices with strategic goals. One of the first areas where this approach bore fruit was in an effort to improve patient access to the Clinic's outpatient clinics.

Says Wadsworth, "For years, we had been getting complaints that patients couldn't get through on our phone lines to make an appointment. So we started tracking wait times, and in one department, we discovered that patients had to wait an average of 2.5 minutes, or about 25 rings, before the call was answered. We established a goal of having appointment phone lines answered within 25 seconds."

According to Wadsworth, by establishing the KPI of answering phones more quickly—setting a specific, measurable goal and then diligently monitoring progress—the department achieved the goal within a few months. It was a powerful example of how relatively simple fixes and focused attention could solve a thorny problem that had far-reaching implications for revenue generation and reputation.

Buoyed by the success of its early initiatives, Cleveland Clinic went on to identify a total of 20 different operational KPIs that affected financial performance. In addition to the speed of answering appointment lines, other KPIs included metrics such as average length of patient stay and average direct cost per case. The method of reporting on these KPIs was a tool that was dubbed the Performance Wheel, or the Wheel for short. The Wheel was a single-page circular graphic that depicted all the KPIs' current performance against targets and previous month's actuals. There was a Wheel for overall Clinic performance as well as individual Wheels for each business unit. The Wheels were prepared for Loop and other senior executives to monitor the Clinic's progress. In the words of one long-time employee: "If it was on the Wheel, it got fixed."

In 1998—in the wake of unexpected operating losses in excess of $70 million—Loop took performance monitoring and accountability a step further by instituting monthly meetings called Continuous Improvement Summits, with Wheels as the primary reporting tools. Employees who attended these Summits recall they took place in a large conference room in the Clinic's executive suite. Loop would sit at the end of a long rectangular table and the Chairmen for each division and several of the Clinic's other top executives would sit around the table as Wheel performance was reviewed for each Chairman in front of his peers.

The Summits and the Wheels certainly got the attention of the executives whose performances were being scrutinized in this way each month, as did Loop's intensity and focus on the smallest details. For executives unprepared to answer questions about their operational and financial performance—and especially negative variances—they could be harrowing experiences. In some employee circles, the Summits became known as "the Viking dinner table" and the Wheels as the "Wheels of Death."

These tools had their desired effect in across-the-board improvement in Cleveland Clinic's operational and financial performance. In 2002, the Clinic began publishing the Wheels on its intranet to speed up distribution. Before long, senior executives were requesting access to performance information on a daily basis, which was provided.

A New Leader for the 21ˢᵗ Century

After 15 years as CEO, Loop retired in 2004 with an impressive list of accomplishments. Not only had Cleveland Clinic achieved growth by every measure, but its culture had been transformed from one characterized by "relaxed camaraderie" to "proactive urgency."[11] The Continuous Improvement Summits and the Performance Wheels—despite the anxiety they caused many people—certainly helped the Clinic make advances in its drive for greater performance accountability among its key executives.

From the outside looking in, however, it appears that Loop was a leader in the mold of Cleveland Clinic's first president, Dr. George Crile: brilliant, driven, and totally dedicated to the Clinic, but also a benevolent autocrat with a command-and-control style of management. In the command-and-control school, leaders lead and followers follow.

This view of Crile is supported by John Clough, a physician and editor-in-chief of Cleveland Clinic Press, in his book on the history of the institution. Clough noted that precisely what Cleveland Clinic's four founders were thinking of, when they formed the Clinic as a medical group, might have gotten lost somewhere along the line. "Over the years, the phrase [act as a unit] has taken on an egalitarian connotation that has become engrained in the organization, expressing the cooperative spirit of group practice," he wrote.

---

[11]John D. Clough, *To Act as a Unit: The Story of the Cleveland Clinic.* 4ᵗʰ ed. (Cleveland: Cleveland Clinic Press, 2004).

"It is most likely that what Crile had in mind . . . was a military 'unit' whose predictable function was assured by the fact that its members were used to following orders," he added.[12]

Command and control was a common management style in America in the 1920s and 1930s and it worked well for Crile. It also was used effectively by Loop in the 1990s and early 2000s—but by then it was showing its age. Command and control is not especially well suited to the increasingly complex and dynamic business environment of the 21st century, which demands the kind of speed and agility that cannot be achieved in environments where people wait to be told what to do.

Also, it certainly doesn't fit the healthcare industry today, which is under severe pressure to reform. Trends such as the rising cost of healthcare and the increasing power of the consumer are forcing providers to become more efficient, transparent, and accountable in how they manage resources and deliver care, which in turn demands greater transparency and accountability internally. This is hard to achieve without the complete engagement of a talented workforce. And, today's workforce—in this age of empowerment—doesn't particularly like being micromanaged or told what to do at every turn.

So while there will always be larger-than-life leaders of heroic proportions, in most healthcare organizations today—indeed, in any organization beyond a certain size—there is just too much for one man or woman to know or do, and the competition is too strong and too relentless for a one-person show. Instead, healthcare organizations need managers and employees who are aligned with the overall objectives and strategies of the organization, feel empowered to act on their own initiative, and take personal responsibility, as well as responsibility as a member of a team, for the organization's results.

---

[12]Ibid. p. 12.

Loop's successor, Dr. Delos "Toby" Cosgrove, appears to be the right kind of leader for this current phase of Cleveland Clinic's journey toward becoming a performance-directed culture. Like Loop before him, Cosgrove spent his entire career at Cleveland Clinic—30 years—as a world-class cardiac surgeon and head of cardiac care before becoming CEO in 2004. His own research produced more than 30 patents. As a result, his credibility with the Clinic's medical staff is high and his commitment to medical excellence is unquestioned.

When Cosgrove became CEO, he inherited a healthcare system much larger and more complex than his predecessors', and at a time when the healthcare industry faces unprecedented challenges. What stands out is his apparent grasp of the demands of managing a modern-day healthcare system. Many of the innovations mentioned at the outset of this chapter—the use of the Internet and social media to improve patient access to information, the electronic medical records pilot program, providing transparency into business relationships that might pose conflicts of interest for Clinic physicians, and the reorganization of the Clinic into multispecialty Institutes—happened on Cosgrove's watch.

Cosgrove also seems equally comfortable with the softer side of medicine. Patient outcomes are paramount, but the totality of patient care at a time when patients are empowered to be discerning consumers of healthcare is top of mind for him as well. One of Cosgrove's innovations is the Office of Patient Experience, which was established in 2007 with an ambitious charter that involves examining every point of contact between the patient and the Clinic—"from parking to prescription pick up." Its aim is to improve every facet of the patient experience, and Cosgrove is one of its most passionate supporters.

And although Cosgrove shares Loop's commitment to formal processes and systems for performance management, there is an all-important difference: While Loop used performance information to ensure compliance with his own personal decisions and strategies, Cosgrove uses it also to empower leaders at all levels of the organization and as a learning tool for everyone in the organization—an essential component of a performance-directed culture.

One way Cosgrove is accomplishing this is by replacing the Performance Wheels with highly intuitive executive dashboards that provide a high-level view of performance on a daily basis across the entire Clinic as well as views customized for each user. The formats of the executive dashboards and each of the customized views are designed for quick interpretation of information. The dashboards are interactive, and by simply clicking on various tabs, users can drill down into more granular views of the information about the performance of their individual business units. The dashboards also serve as a single version of the truth about the overall performance of the entire Clinic.

Because the dashboards are available daily, they enable executives to track and monitor operational performance in near-real time. While this frequency is not necessary for everything, it is valuable for tracking KPIs where immediate intervention could make a difference. For example, through a combination of weekly monitoring of nursing agency expenses and focused and immediate fixes, the Clinic was able to reduce nursing agency expenses from more than $500,000 per month to less than $50,000 per month, for an annual reduction of more than $5 million.

The first dashboards were launched in 2006, and because Cosgrove is considered a "power user," Clinic leaders and managers have taken the time to understand the strategic goals and metrics the dashboards report on and to incorporate their use into their own performance management activities. The Clinic is in the process of executing a comprehensive program of creating and delivering dashboards that report on the Clinic's core KPIs.

Dashboards in production as of this writing include the following: executive; Institute Scorecard; daily census; finance and statistics; service line; patient access; quality; patient experience; blood utilization; and operations dashboards for nursing, hospital operations, clinic operations, physician, and patient support services. Dashboards in development include: ICU; supply chain; revenue cycle; managed care; quality enhancements; workforce management; human resources; treasury/fund reporting; and service line enhancements. Several other dashboards are in the planning stage.

To track progress toward strategic objectives, Cosgrove replaced the monthly Continuous Improvement Summits with quarterly Institute Scorecard meetings with the heads of each Cleveland Clinic Institute. The consistent format of the Scorecard applies the same metrics to all the Institutes, making it easy for everyone to read and interpret them. This also helps ensure alignment throughout the organization.

One interesting side note: While the executive dashboards are clearly Cosgrove's standard performance management tool—and are growing in popularity throughout the Clinic—the Performance Wheels still exist and are still being used by some executives instead of or in addition to the dashboards.

Apparently, at Cleveland Clinic, even the Wheels of Death cling to life.

Cleveland Clinic and the Performance Culture Maturity Model

Despite an 88-year history, Cleveland Clinic's journey on the path to becoming a performance-directed culture really began in earnest 16 years ago. Notable milestones and events since then can be mapped on my Performance Culture Maturity Model to chart its progress (see Figure 3.1).

(Continued)

	Alignment with Mission	Transparency and Accountability	Action on Insights	Conflict Resolution	Common Trust in Data	Availability and Currency of Information
Performance-Directed Culture Realized	Actionable and embraced mission —supported, informed, and reinforced by metrics [2007/9]	General transparency and accountability accepted as cultural tenets [2008]	"Closed loop" processes ensure timely, concerted action	Established and effective mechanisms for resolving conflicts [2009]	Data as truth: Common [2009] application of data, filters, rules, and semantics	Currency of metrics/data matches rhythm of business [2007/9]
Performance-Directed Culture Emerging	Actionable mission supported by "top-down" metrics [2005/6]	Limited [2005/6] transparency and accountability; multiple functions collaborate	Ad hoc [2007/9] (informal) action on insights across functions	When identified, [2007/8] conflicts resolved on an impromptu basis	Common data: [2007/8] Provincial views and semantics used to support specific positions	Enterprise availability, uneven currency of information [2005/6]
Departmental Optimization	Alignment with discrete functional goals, not enterprise mission [2003/4]	Fragmented transparency and accountability within discrete functions [2003/4]	Uncoordinated/ [2003/4] parochial action (sometimes at the expense of others) [2005/6]	Appearance of cooperation, "opportunistic reconciliation" [2003/4]	Conflicting, functional views of data cause confusion, disagreement [2005/6]	Availability and currency [2003/4] directed by departmental sources [2005/6]
Chaos Reigns	Mission not [2003/4] actionable, not communicated, and/or not understood [2000]	Arbitrary accountability, general opacity [2000]	Insights rarely leveraged [2000]	Conflicting, redundant, and competing efforts are the norm [2000]	Data and information generally unreliable and distrusted [2000]	Multiple, inconsistent data sources, conflicting semantics [2000]

FIGURE 3.1 Cleveland Clinic and the Performance Culture Maturity Model[TM]

Source: © 2009 Patent Pending Dresner Advisory Services, LLC

The first phase of the journey began in 1993 and continued until 2003, during which time a data-driven culture emerged at Cleveland Clinic as an outgrowth of efforts to cope with a financial crisis faced by a new CEO in 1989. The second phase lasted from 2003 to 2004, when Medical Operations and Finance began to partner on performance management initiatives that began as separate efforts. The year 2004 marked an important milestone when a new CEO was appointed, who in turn appointed a new CFO.

The third phase occurred in 2005 and 2006, when the joint Medical Operations and Finance initiatives rose in visibility, coming to the attention of the new CEO, who became a champion. In 2005—with the full support of the new CEO—performance management at Cleveland Clinic formally took on strategic importance and began to be resourced more appropriately relative to its importance to the Clinic.

The fourth phase started in 2007 and continues to the present, and is marked by the ongoing enterprise-wide deployment of performance management systems and tools.

Despite what might be considered a long, slow ramp of performance management initiatives at Cleveland Clinic, it's important to keep in mind several facts about the Clinic when evaluating its progress: The Clinic's revenues are rapidly approaching $5 billion, the poor economy notwithstanding; it has 40,000 employees in multiple facilities in far-flung geographies around the world; and its day-to-day management structure is decentralized. Many organizations of this size and complexity never progress beyond departmental performance initiatives, making Cleveland Clinic's achievements all the more impressive.

Phase I: 1993–2002

The year 1993 marked the beginning of Cleveland Clinic's evolution as a data-driven culture. Then-CEO Dr. Floyd Loop

(Continued)

had been able to guide the Clinic through a serious financial crisis by using data manually gathered and reported. But the experience served as the proverbial "wake-up call" to management and prompted Loop to begin a more formal process of establishing KPIs and systematically gathering and reporting data that would enable him to monitor the Clinic's performance against those performance indicators. The primary reporting tool, as mentioned previously, was the one-page report known as a Performance Wheel.

A second financial crisis—considered all the more serious because it was unexpected—occurred in 1998 when the Clinic's operating loss exceeded $70 million. It was during this crisis that Loop commenced his Continuous Improvement Summits, and ongoing analysis of financial and operational performances became a priority at the Clinic. However, due to the often-intimidating nature of these Summits, both they and Performance Wheels earned a negative reputation within the Clinic.

And, in spite of that oasis of performance management, it was quite common for department heads to present conflicting views of performance, and the "gaming" of information was rampant. Typically, whoever presented his or her statistics first was given greater credibility than those who presented later. An especially savvy group of end users, these department heads also were able to cleverly construct queries and create skewed views of data to support their particular agendas.

Says Tom Wadsworth, Senior Director of Medical Operations and Nursing, "We'd go into these Summits and I'd say, 'Well, length of stay is 5.4 days,' and another department would come in the next hour and say, 'No, it's 5.1.'"

Such discrepancies often were based on how the initial data queries were set up. On the question of the length of patient stays, for example, one department might ask that doctors who did minimally invasive surgery be removed because their lengths of stay are very short, while another department might be doing something all-encompassing, requiring longer patient stays. And a third department might ask that length of stays of more than 50 days be excluded from the analysis because they should be considered outliers.

"The problem was we had a culture of people who were savvy enough to ask questions a certain way to get the answers they wanted to take to the Summit," says Wadsworth. "Summits were pretty short and we didn't have time to explain a lot of detail. And, some of these practices were very difficult to explain to a group of top executives who were not as familiar with the data."

Both Medical Operations and Finance participated in these monthly Summits. Each cared about and measured patient access to hospital services. However, while Medical Operations was interested in utilization of resources and patient outcomes, Finance was more concerned with return on assets and profitability. Still, there was a common thread across both and their conflicting views were often a source of frustration for each department, which in its own way was trying to create a single version of the truth about the Clinic's performance.

According to Steve Glass, Cleveland Clinic's current CFO, "If you go back several years, I can remember sitting in the boardroom with Dr. Loop and the administrative council for his direct reports. In those meetings people would bring in information and there would be a huge battle over whose information was right. Finance and Medical Operations were the source of much of that information, but because they were separate departments, each was often unaware that they had been asked to prepare information in different ways for the same meetings. After awhile, Finance and Medical

(Continued)

Operations looked at each other and said, 'We're tired of walking into this room.'"

That frustration would serve as the catalyst for Cleveland Clinic's next stage of evolution.

This was in 2000, and in terms of ranking on Performance Culture Maturity Model, Cleveland Clinic would have to be considered largely departmentally optimized. While senior management was using information on the Wheel to drive the organization's financial performance from the top down, departments were primarily focused on their own interests and used available information to support their own agendas and objectives—which often were aligned with their respective functions and not the enterprise mission.

Phase II:2003–2004

This timeframe marked an important transitional period in Cleveland Clinic's history. Although its performance-directed maturity score improved only modestly during this time, important changes were set in motion. In 2004, Dr. Toby Cosgrove was appointed its new CEO. Not only did he reinvigorate the Clinic's historical mission, "patient first," he encouraged innovative ideas and approaches to problem solving.

In addition, shortly after his appointment, Cosgrove selected Steve Glass as the new CFO. In contrast to the previous CFO, Glass had a good appreciation for Business Intelligence (BI) and its capabilities. During this period, the Performance Wheels continued to evolve, eventually moving to the web for improved access. However, the Continuous Improvement Summits, where the Wheels had served as a centerpiece, were brought to an end.

It was during this period that Medical Operations and Finance developed a closer working relationship and began to share information and collaborate on the reporting of key metrics. By reconciling their views they were able to begin to present a more consistent view to senior management at monthly meetings. According to Andrew Proctor, Administrative Director of Medical Operations, "We knew that because we had so much overlap and we worked together so much, we could at least get on the same page so that people didn't play us off each other. This would avoid the situation where if they didn't like the answer Andrew gave they'd call Chris[13] and try to get a different answer."

Sometime during 2004, Glass presided over a meeting with Medical Operations, Finance, and IT to talk about a broader BI and data warehousing initiative. At the time IT expressed little interest in the initiative and Glass's efforts to expand it beyond Medical Operations and Finance. This was largely due to the IT department's belief that these projects had failed at many places before and its concern about its ability to construct and maintain a large enterprise data warehouse with so much else going on in the organization at that time.

Says Chris Donovan, Senior Director of Fiscal Services, "I think they [IT] had some valid reasons to be kind of worried about where this could go because I think a lot of IT shops have looked very bad spending millions of dollars and not accomplishing anything. So they were a little gun shy to take this on, honestly. And I can understand that; I mean there was no enterprise mandate to do it."

In some ways this may have been a benefit as the two departments working together were able to move more quickly than they might have if they had been forced to adhere to IT processes and standards.

(Continued)

---

[13]Chris Donovan was Proctor's counterpart in Finance.

It was also during this period that Proctor was asked to provide support for Pediatrics, when Dr. Marc Harrison, then-Chairman of Pediatric Critical Care, asked him to help improve the group's performance on the Wheel. It was here that he and Chris Donovan tested their theory: That daily updates to metrics could help improve performance. Once implemented, the daily Wheel helped Pediatrics dramatically improve, which led to a request and funding from the division of surgery for a "physician dashboard." The idea behind this project was to push information to physicians every time they logged on to their computers. This approach of force-feeding information to clinicians was summarily rejected by those physicians, and ultimately discontinued. However, the project provided needed funding for the next stage of BI evolution.

As a result of the appointment of new leadership and the joint efforts between Medical Operations and Finance, Cleveland Clinic moved up on my Maturity Model in the categories of Alignment with Mission, Transparency and Accountability, Action on Insights, Conflict Resolution, and Availability and Currency of Information. However, even though the seeds were sown for substantial improvement, the Clinic's performance initiatives were still predominantly departmentally optimized at this stage.

Phase III:2005–2006

This phase marked significant and real change at Cleveland Clinic. By this time, Cosgrove's new articulation of the Clinic's commitment to patients—"patient first"—had been well communicated throughout the organization and was being used as a tool to drive change. The Clinic's new CFO, Glass, also began to have an impact. A much stronger advocate of BI than his predecessor, Glass learned that answers to key business questions were hard to come by and this spurred him to action.

Donovan describes the transformation this way: "When Steve first got here, we showed him our Green Book[14] that contained all of our key metrics and statistics. When he got to the third page, which included the number of hospital admissions, he started asking questions: 'What's behind that number? I see that it went down, but why? Where did it go down? What area did it go down in? What's driving that?'"

"The book didn't really have any detail," says Donovan. "And so in Finance we had a sense that we needed this information to have more depth and more drilldown functionality. We needed to be able to react more quickly, be more proactive, and not have to wait until the end of the month for data and to take action."

At the same time, according to Proctor, Medical Operations also was interested in more detail and in more timely information. Says Proctor, "They didn't want to know what their speed to answer [the phones] was two weeks after the month's end. They wanted to know during the month so they could get it fixed before the end of the month. An open slot in a physician's appointment book is like a seat on an airplane. Once the flight takes off you can't sell the seat anymore."

During this time, the combined Medical Operations and Finance BI team invested in technology and staff to support its growing efforts. Living outside of the IT environment, the team's system was labeled an "alien application" and was not recognized or supported by the IT staff. So the team recruited and hired technical staff, and contracted with

(Continued)

---

[14]So named because it had a green cover.

external resources to construct and maintain BI applications. Building its own data warehouse, the team began to create and publish dashboards for management consumption. The first dashboard was published in January 2006, followed by several more in a very short span of time.

The most significant was a Patient Access application, which corresponded to a critical CEO initiative—patient access to hospital resources. Realizing that this could be a big win, the team quietly developed a Patient Access dashboard prototype for Cosgrove and his team. Because of its familiarity with the problem, a deep understanding of the underlying data, and its unique approach to metrics, the team was able to deliver exactly what Cosgrove needed.

According to Wadsworth, "When Dr. Cosgrove took over, he said he was tired of hearing out in the community that Cleveland Clinic was a great place to get care if you can get in. So he wanted to tackle access, and specifically outpatient access."

"To support this, we came up with completely new ways to measure patient access," says Proctor. "Instead of trying to come up with one metric, we showed three different ways to look at access, so you can't game the system. That was one thing that Dr. Cosgrove really liked."

According to Donovan, one of the team's "aha" moments was during one of the first Institute Scorecard meetings, when Dr. Cosgrove asked one of the Chairmen: "Why is your black line so far below your green line?" The Chairman replied, "I'm not sure what the green line is."

"It was clear that Dr. Cosgrove understood how to interpret the data in the dashboard and that he was looking at it," says Donovan. "That's when a lot of other people in the Clinic decided they'd better start looking at it, too."

As a result of the effort to improve patient access, wait time for patients seeking an appointment at one of the Clinic's outpatient clinics decreased from 13 days to 8 days.

This meant that an additional 100,000 visits annually could be added to the scheduling system without adding more physicians or support staff.

This success gave the BI team the credibility needed to expand its efforts and convince other groups to collaborate with it. The Patient Access dashboard ultimately evolved into an Institute Scorecard and use of the Scorecard became the basis of Institute reviews with Cosgrove and his Chief of Staff, Dr. Joseph Hahn.

According to Hahn, "We started out doing performance reviews once a quarter with the clinical departments. After a year we had all the other departments saying, 'We want to participate too.' So now we do it over two days and we include everybody. I think people originally went into this wondering, 'Am I going to get my head chopped off?' We made it very clear that we can both learn—we can learn from you, you can learn from us. We can hear what everybody is doing, including best practices, and BI gave us the ability to show people the trend lines and where things were moving. When all the other Institutes asked to be included, I was pleasantly surprised."

In 2005, top management also chartered a bottom-up process reengineering and improvement effort. External resources familiar with lean manufacturing and Six Sigma methodologies were recruited to lead this effort. The resulting Strategic Planning & Continuous Improvement (SPCI) team engaged with specific departments in an effort to streamline processes and improve efficiency. As a byproduct they developed their own metrics and the tools for inputting and viewing them. These metrics were then used to support the "Business Review"—a monthly departmental (later Institute) meeting to evaluate process improvements.

Unfortunately, many of these resulting SPCI metrics overlapped or were redundant with what had been created by

(Continued)

the BI team. And, in many instances, department heads began contacting the BI team to help them populate their SPCI templates with metrics from Performance Wheels or dashboards. This created both confusion and duplicative work.

Nevertheless, during this phase, Cleveland Clinic improved in almost every category on my Maturity Model. In particular, its position for Alignment with Mission, Transparency and Accountability, and Action on Insights rocketed up to Performance-Directed Culture Emerging. This was, in large part, due to the exceptional work of Medical Operations and Finance operating as a BI team and its adoption of a broader and more strategic mission, the creation of the Access prototype, and its ability to successfully demonstrate support for critical CEO initiatives. However, the parallel SPCI initiative and limited IT support held back Cleveland Clinic's progress in other areas.

Phase IV:2007–2009

In 2007, Cleveland Clinic began its reorganization from departments based on functional medical specialties into its current system of multispecialty Institutes organized about diseases or organ systems. Institutes brought related disciplines under a single management structure. For instance, the Heart Institute now includes both cardiologists and cardiac surgeons—improving both synergy and patient care.

By all accounts, this major reorganization brought new blood into the ranks of management that hadn't had exposure to older reporting and measurement systems. As a result, these new managers were open to new tools to help improve performance and were anxious to use the BI dashboards. This was a huge boost to the BI team and enabled it to implement a plan to extend the reach of the performance management initiatives to all of the Institutes. With older discrete views of the Clinic eliminated, Institutes could now manage their performance and view that of their peers across the organization. This created a virtuous cycle within the Clinic and began to change the way that users perceived information and its impact on performance.

According to Marc Harrison, who is now Vice Chairman of Professional Staff Affairs and Director of Medical Operations at Cleveland Clinic, "We have a really long history of using metrics here, so this was an extension of that. But the real beauty of it—the reason why it's gotten so much traction—is we've turned metrics from a bludgeon into a lever. We're providing people with instruments to manage their business in as close to real time as we can get."

It was at this point that the divisional management meetings transitioned to quarterly Institute reviews, with an Institute Scorecard as the underlying mechanism for sharing and communicating performance. According to Glass, "In support of the Institute meetings, there's a tremendous amount of work that gets done to make sure the Institutes are prepared, that they know how to use the tools and have access to the information. When they come in they're extremely prepared, they know what the expectations are going to be from Toby [Cosgrove] and Joe [Hahn], and they're all speaking from the same tabloid of information."

It was during this time that the IT department became a more active participant with the BI team. BI continues to be a shared function and is not "owned" by any one department, but each department now has a specific role: Medical Operations is responsible for the user environment, Finance for the data warehouse, and IT for the management and leverage of operational sources. All three departments participate in BI group management, decision making, and operations.

(Continued)

Also during 2008 and 2009, the BI team began collaborating with the SPCI group. In 2008, for example, the Business Review "deck" was constructed using the BI platform and, in 2009, a consistent Scorecard methodology was adopted across monthly business reviews, bimonthly financial reviews, and quarterly Institute Scorecard reviews. Says Harrison, "We've taken a business review process from the ground up in a number of Institutes and have worked to spread it across all of them in a way that syncs perfectly with what's coming from the top. Front-line people are using data from our dashboards, focused on the right thing to do for their part of the business, but keeping us all pulling in the same direction. So we're one big team from top to bottom: Data informs strategy and strategy informs tactics from both the top and bottom. We could not do that without Business Intelligence."

During this stage, Cleveland Clinic has been able to "put all the pieces together," successfully moving into the Performance-Directed Culture Realized level for nearly all criteria.

That Cleveland Clinic has been a performance-directed culture is remarkable in many ways. As previously mentioned, it's a large and complex organization, and it's impressive that it's been able to achieve an enterprise-level BI implementation—even though the journey took 16 years.

Also unusual is that on their own initiative and for the overall good of the Clinic, Medical Operations and Finance formed what was at first an informal alliance to develop joint BI capabilities. This is extraordinary in that Operations and Finance in most organizations rarely collaborate strategically—and almost never without a mandate from the top.

It is largely due to the passion and commitment of Medical Operations and Finance that Cleveland Clinic now has a fully realized performance-directed culture supported by an enterprise-wide BI system that grows more robust all the time. To underscore this achievement—and the role that BI has played in this transformation—Cleveland Clinic recently formed a new company chartered to sell its BI know-how and solutions to other healthcare organizations around the world. That could well be the subject of a future case study.

CHAPTER 4

Northern California Public Broadcasting

Like most nonprofit organizations, San Francisco-based Northern California Public Broadcasting (NCPB) must strike a balance between activities that directly fulfill its mission and raising enough money to break even. With some notable exceptions—and despite continual fundraising pressure—for much of its 55-year history, NCPB has done a superb job. A pioneer in the public broadcasting community in both local programming and fundraising, NCPB is widely recognized as one of the nation's most innovative and successful public media organizations.

From very humble beginnings—the organization's first office famously was in the back of a station wagon—NCPB today is parent company to public television stations in San Francisco, San Jose, and Watsonville/Monterey; public radio stations in San Francisco and Sacramento; an Education Network (EdNet); and the interactive platforms KQED.org, KQET.com, and KTEH.org.

In its fiscal year 2008,[1] NCPB—better known by the call letters of its flagship television and radio stations, KQED—had more than one million listeners, more than 200,000 members,

---

[1]Ended September 30, 2008.

and revenues of more than $60 million. In May 2009, KQED won five Northern California Emmy Awards from 18 nominations. And, in recent years, KQED Public Television and KQED Public Radio have become the most-watched and the most-listened to public media stations in the country.

For all its accomplishments as a public media company, there is one area where KQED seems to lag. The organization has been slow to embrace a growing trend in the nonprofit world: applying world-class management techniques, processes, and systems honed in for-profit enterprises to achieve break-through performance—the kind of performance that enables nonprofits to thrive regardless of economic downturns or changes in the fundraising climate.

Of course, this is easier said than done. For starters, it's not enough for nonprofits to simply adopt for-profit business practices. Many for-profit businesses are poorly run and are not great role models.

In addition, while nonprofits and for-profits have many characteristics in common, there are some important differences. Many nonprofits must serve two stakeholders with very different needs: the people who benefit from the services they provide and the people who fund the organization (although in some cases, they are one and the same). In contrast, many for-profits have the advantage of being able to focus on serving just one—the customer who buys the company's product or service. By satisfying its customers, for-profits generally meet the needs of their other stakeholders (although for-profits, too, can be pulled in opposite directions by customers on the one hand and investors on the other).

Another difference often cited is that nonprofits are mission-driven, and can face tough choices between activities that advance their mission and those that produce financial rewards. In all but the worst of financial times, most nonprofits will put mission first—and rightly so, according to many nonprofit management experts, including the most famous management expert in America, Peter F. Drucker.[2] In contrast, most for-profits are driven by their business purpose and—to quote Drucker—"There is only one valid definition of business purpose: to create a customer."[3]

The takeaway is that mission and money can be at odds in nonprofits, while in for-profits, the purpose of the business is nearly always aligned with delivering products or services designed to make money.

Can the Same Standards Be Applied to Nonprofits and For-Profits?

The degree to which these and other differences between nonprofits and for-profits matter when it comes to management is a topic of much debate. Les Silverman and Lynn Taliento, co-founders of McKinsey & Company's Global Nonprofit Practice, believe that even though the gap in understanding between nonprofits and for-profits is narrowing, business leaders continually "underestimate" the unique challenges of managing nonprofit organizations. Silverman and Taliento explored this premise in a 2006 article, "What Business Execs Don't Know—But Should—About Nonprofits,"[4] that included interviews with 11 executives with experience in both types of organizations.

---

[2]Peter F. Drucker, *Managing the Nonprofit Organization* (first published in 1990).

[3]Peter F. Drucker, *Management: Tasks, Responsibilities, Practices*, (New Brunswick and London: Transaction Publishers, 1973).

[4]Les Silverman and Lynn Taliento, "What Business Execs Don't Know—But Should—About Nonprofits," *Stanford Social Innovation Review* (Summer 2006).

One of the executives, William Novelli, is a former consumer packaged goods marketer who built Porter Novelli into one of the largest and most respected public relations firms in the world before serving for eight years as CEO of AARP,[5] a nonprofit, non-partisan membership organization that helps people 50 and over improve the quality of their lives. Said Novelli of the differences between leading a nonprofit and a for-profit organization, "It's harder to succeed in the nonprofit world. For starters, nonprofits' goals are both more complex and more intangible. It may be hard to compete in the field of consumer packaged goods or electronics or high finance, but it's harder to achieve goals in the nonprofit world because these goals tend to be behavioral. If you set out to do something about breast cancer in this country, or about Social Security insolvency, it's a hell of a lot harder to pull that off. And it's also harder to measure."

James A. Phills, Jr., Co-Director of the Center for Social Innovation at Stanford and a faculty member of the Stanford Graduate School of Business, acknowledges the special challenges of nonprofits, but cautions nonprofit executives and managers not to hide behind them. In his book, *Integrating Mission and Strategy for Nonprofit Organizations*,[6] he wrote, "[It] is important to avoid broad generalizations about the differences between nonprofits and businesses, that mask or ignore fundamental similarities with respect to the central management and leadership challenges."

Specifically on the question of whether nonprofits have moved quickly enough to adopt management practices taken for granted in for-profit businesses, Phills noted that "penetration

---

[5]When Novelli resigned in March 2009, AARP had more than 40 million members and an annual budget of $1.2 billion.

[6]James A. Phills, Jr., *Integrating Mission and Strategy for Nonprofit Organizations* (New York: Oxford University Press, 2005). Page 9

and adoption have been hampered by psychological barriers that have less to do with the validity, relevance, or utility of these ideas than with the social significance of their adoption. For example, many fields within the nonprofit sector have long viewed corporate America as an adversary, the embodiment of greed and self-interest, and as a major contributor to social ills such as inequality, rampant consumerism, and environmental degradation. Hence, ideas associated with the business world have been viewed with suspicion in the social sector."[7]

The prose may not sparkle, but Phills's insights shine a light on two fundamental questions about KQED and whether it has achieved a performance-directed culture: First, is it fair to judge KQED by the same criteria used to evaluate the performance management approaches of for-profit companies? In this book, the answer is yes—for the most part.

Second, where KQED falls short, could part of the problem be a lack of trust and stylistic differences between people in the organization focused on KQED's mission as a nonprofit public media company and others from the business world determined to improve its financial processes and systems? For the answer to this question—stay tuned.

Setting the Stage for Public Broadcasting in America

The history of public television in America is a classic tale of a clash between powerful commercial interests and citizens concerned about the public good. By all accounts, the hero of this story (or villain, depending on your perspective) is Frieda Hennock, the first woman to serve as a Commissioner of the Federal Communications Commission (FCC). Appointed by President Harry Truman, she served from 1948 to 1955—a

---

[7]Ibid. Page viii.

time when television was in its infancy in America and the FCC was struggling to sort out how to allocate channels across a finite spectrum.

A practicing attorney in New York City at the time of her confirmation, Hennock became a staunch advocate of setting aside channels for noncommercial television and, more specifically, for educational television. Commercial broadcasting entities argued against such set-asides, saying they were unnecessary—and many FCC Commissioners seemed to agree. Still, Hennock waged a fierce campaign both inside the FCC and publicly in the media in favor of them.

After several attempts over several years—and with the odds stacked against her—Hennock prevailed and, in 1952, the FCC set aside 242 specific channels for noncommercial stations. On May 25, 1953, KUHT-TV in Houston, Texas, became the first educational television station in the country to go on the air. Based at the University of Houston, its first broadcast was a variety show called *It's Five*, which featured college coeds offering advice for women, including tips on makeup, giving parties, and flower arranging.[8]

At the same time, plans were underway at colleges and universities, and in communities all over America—including San Francisco—to establish television stations to take advantage of the FCC ruling.

To no one's surprise, Hennock's term as a Commissioner was not renewed.

San Francisco's Unique Brand of Public Television

San Francisco's reputation as America's capital of counterculture dates back to the 1950s, when the prevailing view was that

---

[8]"50 Years of HoustonPBS History," www.houstonpbs.org.

stability and prosperity could be achieved by living life according to a prescribed set of rules and respect for authority. Not
everyone aspired to such a life, however, and during the early
1950s, like-minded poets, writers, and others were drawn to San
Francisco by its strong support for the arts and their shared dis-
content with the mainstream values of middle-class America at
mid-century.[9]

It was in this atmosphere of creativity and growing
rebellion—sandwiched between the California State Supreme
Court's ruling in 1950 that a bar could not be closed down
because it catered to homosexuals and Allen Ginsberg's famous
reading of his epic Beat poem, "Howl," in 1955—that KQED was
born.

Founded by the Bay Area Educational Television Association, a group of educators, librarians, and directors of
cultural institutions, KQED was meant originally to broadcast
instructional content into schools. Only after incorporating, and
claiming the channel set aside by the FCC for educational use
in San Francisco, did the group learn that the state of California
prohibited schools from using television for instruction.

Apparently undaunted, cofounders Jonathan Rice, a former
news director at a commercial TV station in Los Angeles, and
James Day, a former public affairs and education executive
at a commercial TV station in San Francisco, instead organized KQED as a community rather than educational channel.
KQED's first broadcast—a test pattern—occurred on April 2,
1954, making KQED the sixth public television station to go on
the air in America. Rice would serve as KQED's program director for 25 years and on its board for another 18 years beyond

---

[9]This migration became a movement and its participants were called
the "Beat Generation" by the popular media, a term that was, by
many accounts, coined by writer Jack Kerouac in 1948.

that. Day was KQED's President and General Manager for 16 years.

KQED's early days were lean. From its previously mentioned inaugural "office" in Rice's station wagon, in 1954 KQED acquired a transmitter and a tiny studio atop the Mark Hopkins Hotel, and began broadcasting two nights a week. Programming consisted mainly of taped programs on science and nature.

That same year, KQED launched *Kaleidoscope*, a weekly live series featuring in-depth interviews with important figures of the day. Conceived of and hosted by cofounder Day, it set a signature tone and style for public television interviews. When Day died in 2008, KQED's current President and Chief Executive Officer Jeff Clarke said, "If you look at Dick Cavett, Charlie Rose, William F. Buckley—they all followed the one-on-one format in public broadcasting that James was doing."[10]

The program ran until Day's departure from KQED in 1968 and included interviews with such luminaries as Eleanor Roosevelt, Buster Keaton, Robert Kennedy, Aldous Huxley, Bing Crosby, Maurice Chevalier, Ella Fitzgerald, and Ogden Nash.

After a move to a larger studio in 1955, KQED stepped up its live programming. Energized by the opportunity—but sometimes desperate to fill its growing number of broadcast hours—KQED at first added to its lineup a hodge-podge of shows featuring experts on a variety of subjects from typing and speed-reading to gardening.

By 1957, though, KQED was producing landmark public television. Highlights of that year included *The Elements*, with Nobel laureate Dr. Glenn Seaborg; a debate on nuclear fallout and disarmament in which Nobel-winning biochemist Linus Pauling and H-bomb architect Edward Teller took part;

---

[10]Justin Berton, "James Day—Co-Founder of KQED TV—Dies," *San Francisco Chronicle*, April 30, 2008.

and *Japanese Brush Painting,* in which host Takahiko Mikami demonstrated how to paint fish, bamboo, pine trees, roosters, and other images common in Japanese painting.[11]

To everyone's surprise, *Japanese Brush Painting* became a smash hit, both locally and nationally.[12] The story goes that KQED had put together some brush painting kits so viewers could paint along with Mikami during the show, which it offered for sale for $3.00 each. When thousands of viewers placed orders, the station had to scramble to find enough supplies to fill them, eventually making an agreement with a new airline flying to Japan to bring back kits in exchange for on-air credit.[13]

Despite the exhilarating chaos of those early years—perhaps even because of it—KQED continued to innovate in live and local programming. Over the years, the content it produced uniquely captured the times and the particular sensibilities of San Francisco, and even now sets the standard for public television in America.

Among its most notable productions are:

- 1960: *Photography: The Incisive Art*, a five-part series hosted by Ansel Adams
- 1964: *Where Is Jim Crow?*, a series on San Francisco Bay Area black culture
- 1973: *An American Family*, a 12-hour documentary, which drew a staggering 10 million viewers, featuring the Louds of

---

[11]David Stewart, "KQED Made Its Mark by Making Programs," *Current* (originally published February 3, 1997).

[12]Back then, if a public television station wanted to send a program to other stations, it recorded it using kinescope, a technique of filming television images on a monitor, and sent it via a National Educational Television distribution point in Michigan.

[13]David Stewart, "KQED Made Its Mark by Making Programs," *Current* (originally published February 3, 1997).

Santa Barbara, California, during a time when Bill and Pat Loud were divorcing; according to PBS,[14] the Loud's oldest son, Lance, was the first openly gay person to appear on television as an integral member of an American family's life

- 1986: *South Africa Under Siege*, the account of a group of KQED filmmakers' visit to Zambia to interview exiled leaders of the African National Congress, the leading opponent of apartheid
- 1993: *Tales of the City*, a six-part miniseries based on books by San Francisco author Armistead Maupin; produced in cooperation with Britain's Channel 4 Television Corporation and PBS's *American Playhouse*, the series was controversial for its gay themes, nudity, and illicit drug use, and was one of PBS's highest rated dramatic programs ever
- 2003: *Spark*, a series on the Bay Area arts scene and the first KQED programming to combine content for television and the web with educational outreach
- 2007: *Quest*, a Bay Area science, nature, and environmental series and the largest multiple-media content offering in KQED's history; the series includes a half-hour weekly high-definition (HD) television show, weekly radio segments, a web site, and education guides

In addition to high-quality programming, KQED expanded its services over the years to include radio, first in San Francisco, and then in Sacramento; added programming to cover a full seven-day television schedule; established the Center for Education & Lifelong Learning; and went online with its first web site. In 2006, KQED Inc., as it was then constituted, merged

---

[14]"About the Film: Lance Loud! A Death in an American Family," www.pbs.org/lanceloud/about/, 2001.

with the KTEH Foundation Inc., licensee of a public television station in San Jose, to form Northern California Public Broadcasting Inc. KTEH also brought with it a public television station in Watsonville (KQET) that serves the greater Monterey area, to complete the KQED family of today.

KQED radio was popular from the beginning, but earned its current stellar reputation starting in August 1987, when it changed from a classical music station to an around-the-clock, in-depth news and public affairs station. Two years later, KQED radio was put to the test when, at 5:04 p.m. on October 17, 1989, the Loma Prieta earthquake struck the San Francisco Bay Area. Lasting just 15 seconds, the 6.9 magnitude earthquake killed 63 people, injured nearly 4,000, and left thousands more homeless. Because the earthquake occurred during the warm-up for the third game of the World Series, it was the first earthquake in America broadcast on live television.

Within two hours of the quake, KQED radio was back on the air, thanks to the heroic efforts of Chief Engineer Fred Krock,[15] who drove to the transmitter atop Mt. San Bruno, a few miles south of San Francisco, and worked nonstop for 48 hours. The makeshift system he set up enabled reporters to broadcast from the field. In addition, Krock got frequent updates from the KQED newsroom, which he personally broadcast every 15 minutes.

According to KQED, many San Francisco newspaper columnists reported that their first news about the quake came from KQED radio. Even one of UC Berkeley's seismologists learned of the quake from KQED radio. He was listening to the station at the exact moment the quake struck and heard the announcer

---

[15]This account of the aftermath of the earthquake appears in the 1980s KQED History on the KQED web site, www.kqed.org/about/history/1980s.jsp.

say, "Wow, that's a big one; the whole studio's shaking!" A
second later, it hit Berkeley.[16]

Seismic Changes in Public Broadcasting

For the first 15 years of public television in America, even
though they shared programming, individual stations had to go it
alone with funding from private sources. The landscape of public broadcasting changed dramatically when President Lyndon
Johnson signed into law the Public Broadcasting Act of 1967.
The Act provided government funding and called for the forma-
tion of the Corporation for Public Broadcasting (CPB) to ensure
development of and access to high-quality noncommercial programming and telecommunications services.

In 1969, PBS was formed as a private nonprofit organization with funding from the government and its members, which
are America's public TV stations. Its mission was to distribute
programming and related services to its members. In 1973, the
stations expanded that mission to include selecting and, later,
producing programs. PBS today has 356 member stations in
all 50 states and the U.S. territories of Puerto Rico, U.S. Virgin
Islands, Guam, and American Samoa.

NPR, a private nonprofit organization that produces and dis-
tributes radio programming, was founded in 1970.

Equally dramatic for its impact on public broadcasting,
broadcast technology had evolved and changed over the
decades as well. KQED was quick to adopt new technologies but, like most stations, was constrained financially from
making progress as rapidly as it wanted. In 1998, KQED
launched a $70 million Campaign for the Future to pay for the

---

[16]"Looking Back at the Loma Prieta Earthquake," UC Berkeley
    Seismological Laboratory (1999).

government-mandated but unfunded conversion to digital technology and to develop TV and radio programming that could take advantage of it. The more than $74 million raised during this campaign enabled KQED to broadcast its first HDTV signal in 2000 and launch five new digital channels in 2003.

KQED reached its Campaign for the Future fundraising goal in 2004 and replaced all of its analog production and broadcast equipment for radio and television with digital equipment. From a labor-intensive, manual, single-channel analog operation, KQED was transformed into a highly automated multichannel digital HD operation.[17] Today, KQED's flagship station in San Francisco "central-casts" six channels of digital programming to viewers as well as programming for its sister stations in San Jose and Watsonville.

In addition, KQED now has a multiplatform capability that enables it to deliver content across multiple platforms, including television, radio, and the web. KQED's groundbreaking *Quest* science and nature series relies on this multiplatform capability and serves as a model for future programming.

Money Is Always an Issue

Raising $74.3 million—as KQED did during its Campaign for the Future—is a remarkable accomplishment and testimony to KQED's loyal donors and fundraising skills. But in reality, money—or, more precisely, the lack of it—has been a significant problem for KQED from the very beginning. Cofounder Day, in his book, *The Vanishing Vision*,[18] wrote that KQED's

---

[17]"Tech One on One with NTC's Ethan Bush," *TVNEWSDAY*, July 26, 2007.

[18]James Day, *The Vanishing Vision: The Inside Story of Public Television* (Berkeley: University of California Press, 1995).

first year was almost its last. The organization was barely hanging on financially, and distressed by its increasing debt, its board voted to cease operations.

According to Day, he persuaded the board to give him a month to raise more money and, with a few thousand dollars donated by friends, he hired a public relations firm. The firm suggested to Day that KQED host a 24-hour live TV auction, an idea that at the time struck him as crazy. But with no other choice, the auction went forward—and it was wildly successful. It was also an idea that gradually morphed into the public broadcast pledge drive—today a mainstay of fundraising for public media.

Soon thereafter, KQED received a grant from the Ford Foundation, which was the primary funder of educational television until CPB and PBS were formed in the late 1960s.[19] Over the next few years, KQED pioneered a number of other innovative fundraising ideas in attempts to stay solvent—including the concept of offering memberships, which has been adopted by public broadcasting stations all over the country.

Still, several more times in its history, KQED has been forced to take dramatic and sudden action to raise money, cut costs, and improve efficiencies to solve a financial crisis. Some of KQED's financial troubles were the result of external forces beyond its control—for example, when PBS funding stalled in Congress in 1971, and then in the following year when President Richard Nixon vetoed a bill that would have provided funding for the next two years. Other times, KQED's financial woes were the result of ill-advised management decisions sometimes combined with bad luck. Such was apparently

---

[19]All told, the Ford Foundation awarded $290 million in grants in the
    1950s, 1960s, and 1970s to get public stations on the air and
    support the production of high-quality educational programming.

the case in 1992, when KQED found itself on the brink of bankruptcy.

An account of KQED's financial situation published in *Current* at the time described how an unexpected $3.5 million shortfall in membership—caused by delays in sending out renewal notices—combined with the failure of a real estate deal had created a "fiscal crisis" at KQED.[20] The year before, KQED had moved into a new headquarters building, but the sale of its old building fell through, leaving KQED with an additional deficit of $4 million. Against planned revenues of $32 million, a cash shortfall of nearly $8 million was potentially catastrophic.

Executive pay cuts, staff reductions, and huge cutbacks in the locally produced programming that KQED was famous for stemmed some of the losses, but did not make up for them entirely. Then-CEO of KQED, Tony Tiano, was already under attack for a number of controversial actions and decisions. Considered worst of all, Tiano was blamed for lies KQED told to the FCC about why it had shut down a second station it had in San Francisco. KQED told the FCC that it had shut down the station for technical reasons, but the truth was KQED didn't have enough money to operate it. As a result of this incident, the FCC revoked KQED's license for the station.

By the spring of 1993, Tiano was gone, and was replaced by Mary Bitterman, who previously had been Executive Director of the Hawaii Broadcasting Authority. Bitterman's eight-year tenure as CEO was not without its controversy,[21] but she is widely credited with taking KQED from the brink of bankruptcy "to sound financial health, renewed community support, a

---

[20]Steve Behrens, "Revenue Shortfalls Compound KQED's Problems," *Current* (originally published November 16, 1992).

[21]John Carman, "KQED Loses Its Leader," *San Francisco Chronicle*, November 9, 2001.

renaissance in program development, and a strategy for a digital future."[22]

Says Jeff Clarke, KQED's current CEO and Bitterman's immediate successor, of that time, "It was just a mess. When Mary Bitterman came in, she essentially had to rebuild KQED out of the ashes. There were literally times when KQED wasn't sure it could meet payroll, things were that dire. Mary brought the culture back, got it repaired, and got the station back on track with some of the major players in the community."

Following Bitterman's departure, KQED's board hired Clarke after a national search. At the time a 37-year veteran of broadcasting—with more than 24 years in public broadcasting—Clarke was CEO and General Manager of KUHT, HoustonPBS—as previously mentioned, the nation's first public television station. At KUHT, Clarke recently had led a successful capital campaign to support digital conversion—similar to KQED's Campaign for the Future. He joined KQED midway through the campaign and recalls that he spent the vast majority of his time for the first 18 months raising the $30 million needed to complete it.

Since coming to KQED, Clarke, too, has faced his share of financial setbacks. In 2003, an ailing economy forced KQED to lay off staffers for the first time since Bitterman had done it in 1995, and to implement other cost-cutting measures necessary to reduce KQED's budget by $4 million.[23]

Says Clarke of the experience, "Our approach was different from what it had been in the past. We didn't just walk around handing out pink slips. We actually had conversations

---

[22]"Mary Bitterman Leaves KQED Public Broadcasting to Head Irvine Foundation; Led KQED's Resurgence during Eight-Year Tenure," *KQED* press release, November 8, 2001.

[23]Peter Hartlaub, "Cash-Squeezed KQED Cuts Staff, Trims Hours," *San Francisco Chronicle*, July 30, 2003.

and a transparent process that we went through. Management still made the final decisions, but we brought everybody into the conversation. We got the unions involved and everyone bought into a program of early departure packages and vacating a number of unfilled positions. But the key element was we all took a 10% pay cut for 14 months. That meant that we only had to eliminate a small number of jobs.

"The philosophy was, how do you protect the best interests of the organization as well as the people who work here?" adds Clarke. "Because that's one of our core values ... we value our employees and we want to be open, honest, and direct. ... [We're] in the communications business and if we can't be communicative and talk about what the issues are and be upfront about it, how are we going to keep people engaged and productive?"

In the current recession, KQED has been hit hard yet again. While membership numbers have remained high, revenue from major donors, foundations, corporations, and KQED's endowment is down, according to Clarke. And in February 2009, KQED was forced to make budget cuts—including staff reductions—and organizational and structural changes to save approximately $8 million. No small feat for an organization with an annual budget of approximately $60 million.

A Growing Desire for Stronger Financial Management

The majority of nonprofits struggle to maintain their financial health during economic downturns and the vagaries of funding sources. The trend referred to earlier of nonprofits adopting for-profit management processes and systems—which typically involves putting in place better financial controls, among other things—is, in part, designed to help them better weather these inevitable ups and downs.

At KQED, under Clarke, three examples of efforts to do this are a 2003 board-driven strategic planning process that produced an updated plan that effectively operationalized KQED's mission; the hiring of a new CFO in 2006 chartered to remake KQED's financial planning, management, and reporting systems; and the hiring of a facilitator in 2007 to work on team building with KQED's executive management.

According to Clarke, one of the most important things that emerged from the strategic planning process, which resulted in a comprehensive plan in 2004 that was updated again in 2008, is a focus on person hours as a performance metric for KQED. Says Clarke, "If you are someone who listens to the radio for an hour, watches TV for an hour, is involved in our education arena for an hour, or is on our web site for an hour, we count that as four person hours in total."

"The reason we went to that as a measurement is because if you only look at how many people watched or how long they watched, you don't get the total picture of the impact we are having," said Clarke. "Once you track person hours, you can juxtapose person hour gains against the efficiency of the costs of delivering a person hour. For example, when we started out in 2004, we were doing about 110,000 person hours in the education arena. Today that's up to over 350,000. Back then, it was costing us $7.50 to do a person hour in education; we're doing it now for less than $5.00 a person hour."

Of the management team-building initiative, Clarke says, "I brought in an executive coach to work with our management team because I really wanted our team to become more engaged as a team. We've brought in a lot of new people and you've got to get everyone to come together. We're still working on that, but we've learned a lot more about each other and how we think."

One of the things Clarke says he learned during the management team-building exercises is that he is the "only one" on the management team "who looks at a landscape, makes an assessment, and has a sense of what we need to do and where we need to go."

In contrast, according to Clarke, his management team includes mostly individuals who are more analytical. "What they have to do is help me hold back so I can get more data to have a better informed decision," he says. "The process of working together over a period of a year or so has really helped us build a stronger cohesive team."

New CFO Shakes Things Up

Of all the efforts to strengthen KQED's management practices in the 2000s, the one with the most impact—both positive and negative—was the hiring of CFO Jeff Nemy. Nemy was then a 25-year veteran of finance with years of experience in broadcasting, advertising, and consulting—all of it in for-profit businesses such as Chronicle Broadcasting Company, parent of five TV stations including KRON-TV in San Francisco; Foote, Cone & Belding, a multinational advertising agency; the Interpublic Group of Companies, one of the world's largest advertising and marketing services holding companies; and Nextel Communications. Early in his career, he was a management consultant with Arthur Young and Price Waterhouse.

Of Nemy's hiring, Clarke says, "I'm the kind of person who doesn't need 20 pages of material to look at the landscape, but I need to have three pages that are absolutely accurate. I'm not saying we didn't get that before, but there was probably a little more slippage than we could afford ... not only from the standpoint of being able to make good decisions, but just really knowing exactly where we were at any given time."

Nemy arrived at KQED in August 2006, two months before the merger of KQED with its San Jose counterpart, KTEH, was officially completed. An account of his first impressions, published in *CFO* magazine in December 2008 and confirmed by Nemy in interviews, reads like every CFO's worst nightmare: "That would complicate budgeting in the best of times, but Nemy soon found out that it was worse than he feared. When he asked for a copy of the current forecast, he learned there wasn't one. Worse, creating one would require the consolidation of approximately 600 spreadsheets from nearly 200 business units."[24]

Nemy is quoted, "Consolidating all those spreadsheets was going to take up to six weeks. It almost made me walk out the door."

In interviews, Nemy also noted that KQED engaged in an annual planning cycle that took as long as five months each year and that resulted in a budget that looked out only over the next fiscal year. In other words, KQED had almost no visibility into its expected or desired financial performance beyond 12 months out.

Nemy didn't walk out the door, though, and instead plowed through the process of producing a budget for the merger. He then initiated a search for a business planning and consolidation software system that would provide rolling 36-plus month forecasts and automate the mostly manual processes at KQED. After finding and purchasing one, he kicked off its implementation in March 2007, determined to get out ahead of the next annual planning cycle that would begin in May.

To meet this deadline, Nemy developed a fast-track implementation plan based on two key assumptions: (1) that users, mostly department heads and managers, already were analyzing their monthly financial reports and understood revenue and expense account recognition; and (2) that users understood

---

[24]Russ Banhan, "Cutting Through the Static," *CFO* (December 2008).

Excel well enough to use it as their primary tool for entering data. In hindsight, according to Nemy, these two assumptions were "optimistic."

Moreover, because of the short development and implementation time and limited budget, defining user needs and testing were not as comprehensive as Nemy would have liked.

Repercussions from the fast-track implementation linger throughout KQED in the form of a lack of trust in the data and reports produced by the system, and persistent resistance among some key members of the management team to using the system the way the development team envisioned. It is striking to hear some key executives and managers at KQED—nearly two years after the financial management system went live—describe their interactions with the system as something they do "for Finance." The unspoken—but crystal clear—implication is that they still do not see its benefits to their own function or to the overall organization.

Of the way the financial management system was implemented and introduced within KQED, Clarke says, "If we had to do it over again, I would have asked Jeff [Nemy] to wait to implement, to take more time to implement the new system. I think that caused more difficulty because we were doing multiple things at the same time. We were consummating a merger, doing a new budget, putting in a new system, all in the course of a four- or five-month period. So there were a lot of issues and you probably heard somewhere of people putting data in and having it disappear or putting data in and getting stuff back that they didn't think was right."

The system is now fully operational, with the problems that surfaced during its initial implementation phase largely resolved. Usage within the organization has increased while resistance has decreased. And, Nemy, along with his management colleagues, recently created a Financial Services Group within Finance to provide all department and project heads consistent "cradle to grave" financial management services, including inputting data and producing and interpreting reports.

For his part, Nemy is genuinely surprised that some people at KQED—including some key executives—still have such negative feelings about the system. To him, it's "obvious" that what the system brings to KQED is what any organization should have in order to better manage its finances, improve visibility into the state of its financial health, and make better data-driven decisions.

Which brings us back full circle to the second question posed at the outset of this profile: Could part of the problem at KQED be a lack of trust and stylistic differences between people in the organization focused on its mission as a nonprofit public media company and others from the business world determined to improve its financial processes and systems? Even though all players in this organizational drama seem completely dedicated to KQED—and are pursuing its mission with the very best of intentions from their own different vantage points—the answer is yes.

Which leads to yet another question: Will KQED be able to bridge this cultural divide and become a fully realized performance-directed culture across all its functional areas and in all of its endeavors?

As before, for the answer, we will have to stay tuned.

KQED and the Performance Culture Maturity Model

KQED is, by most standards, a very successful organization. One of the nation's foremost public broadcasting concerns, KQED produces some of the finest content in the public broadcasting system and is passionately committed to its mission and community.

Even so, as I met and spoke with its employees, I discovered a culture that is relatively low on the Performance Culture Maturity Model scale (see Figure 4.1).

I also observed the changes that are afoot at KQED. Increasingly, the organization has been forced to operate more like a business and provide greater transparency into its use of donor funds. This has created a sort of clash of cultures between the mission-driven and business-driven elements within KQED. Mission-driven employees seek the freedom to produce the content they perceive the community wants and needs, while business-driven employees want to manage and control costs.

Says Jeff Clarke of this apparent dichotomy, "Content is always going to be Number One. That's our business. However, it's easier to raise money when you're good stewards and can actually show how efficient you are; it's easier to do what you're doing if you know in advance what it's really going to take to do it."

And, according to Suzanne Romaine, Director of KQED Presents, "Our mission is about making media, not budgets. I'm concerned about our ability to remain focused on our mission while implementing a system of centralized decision making that is driven by people whose jobs are about creating budgets."

This tension is representative of growing pains that eventually may lead to a happy medium with the emergence of an organization that is both mission-driven and performance-oriented.

Because the effort to put in place more stringent management processes and systems on the financial side of KQED is so new, it's more instructive to look at how KQED stacks up by attribute rather than in chronological phases.

(Continued)

	Alignment with Mission	Transparency and Accountability	Action on Insights	Conflict Resolution	Common Trust in Data	Availability and Currency of Information
Performance-Directed Culture Realized	Actionable and embraced mission—supported, informed, and reinforced by metrics [2009]	General transparency and accountability accepted as cultural tenets	"Closed loop" processes ensure timely, concerted action	Established and effective mechanisms for resolving conflicts	Data as truth: Common application of data, filters, rules, and semantics	Currency of metrics/data matches rhythm of business
Performance-Directed Culture Emerging	Actionable mission supported by "top-down" metrics [2006]	Limited transparency and accountability; multiple functions collaborate	Ad hoc (informal) action on insights across functions [2009]	When identified, conflicts resolved on an impromptu basis	Common data: Provincial views and semantics used to support specific positions [2009]	Enterprise availability, uneven currency of information
Departmental Optimization	Alignment with discrete functional goals, not enterprise mission	Fragmented transparency and accountability within discrete functions [2009]	Uncoordinated/parochial action (sometimes at the expense of others) [2006]	Appearance of cooperation, "opportunistic reconciliation" [2009] [2006]	Conflicting, functional views of data cause confusion, disagreement [2009] [2006]	Availability and currency [2009] directed by departmental sources [2006]
Chaos Reigns	Mission not actionable, not communicated, and/or not understood	Arbitrary accountability, general opacity [2006]	Insights rarely leveraged	Conflicting, redundant, and competing efforts are the norm	Data and information [2007] generally unreliable and distrusted	Multiple, inconsistent data sources, conflicting semantics [2006]

FIGURE 4.1 KQED and the Performance Culture Maturity Model[TM]

Source: © 2009 Patent Pending Dresner Advisory Services, LLC

Alignment with Mission

In this category, KQED shines. Its official mission statement reads: "NCPB provides consistently high-quality, public media that informs, educates, entertains, and engages from a Northern California perspective."

According to Clarke, "Over our history we've had an opportunity to connect with the community in a wide array of ways, that is considered, one of the beacons within our industry and in this community. It ranks on a par with the symphony, the ballet, the opera, and museums; it's really a cut above where public broadcasting institutions generally rank in their communities."

The people of KQED are passionate about public broadcasting and KQED. In fact, so inspired by KQED's mission and its status as a cultural institution of high regard, in some instances, employees have chosen to leave commercial enterprises, taking significant pay cuts, to join KQED.

As I met with various employees, it became clear that KQED has a well-conceived, understood, embraced, and actionable mission. Everyone understands the mission and, with few exceptions, is well aligned. In addition, the strategic plan that was implemented first in 2004 and updated in 2007 contains specific metrics such as "content hours" and "cost of reach," which, if achieved, will significantly enhance overall support for KQED's mission. As a result, I rank KQED's Alignment with Mission as "emerging," but right on the cusp of Performance-Directed Culture Realized, a very impressive accomplishment.

There is an opportunity that, however, in my opinion, is being overlooked. KQED's impressive alignment with its membership and community ought to be used as a means for driving needed change in financial and operational areas

(Continued)

as well as content. Financial initiatives viewed through the filter of "community first," or even "member first," might be much more well received than they are now.

Transparency and Accountability

In contrast with its outstanding alignment with mission, KQED suffers from limited Transparency and Accountability. Although there are various sources of information that are used, they tend to be limited to departments or functions. For instance, the Business Development function has its membership database in an application called Team Approach. The data in this Customer Relationship Management (CRM)-type system for public broadcasting is sent to Target Analytics once a year for analysis. The resulting analysis is returned in hard and soft copy and is then used daily to help benchmark performance with peers in the industry.

However, this information is not broadly shared throughout the organization. Syndicated sources (Arbitron for radio and Nielsen for TV) are subscribed to but not widely distributed outside the subscribing department. These sources are not online for other managers to access directly and cannot be combined with other sources for a more complete view of the business. Additionally, Operations has its own data—which tracks programming and utilization of various production assets—that is not made available outside its own department.

In fact, the only source of information that is available across the organization comes from Finance.

In 2006, with board and CEO support, CFO Jeff Nemy chose to implement a more modern budgeting and forecasting system with the intent of establishing better fiscal controls and predictability. According to Nemy, "When I was hired one of the things that board members talked to me about was being able to figure out what's really going on. For *Ocean Adventures*,[25] for example, we booked $2 million in October when we got our grant and we had no expenses. So for that fiscal year, it looks like we're brilliant.

"But it's not until the next fiscal year that all those costs are going to hit," continued Nemy. "If you don't have a good way to manage it, you could easily go right off the edge. Our objective is not to make money; we just don't want to lose money and we want to have maximum impact on the screen."

Prior to the new system, all budgeting was accomplished using spreadsheets, which was cumbersome, inefficient, and error-prone. A tool was chosen and quickly implemented before the 2007 budgeting cycle ensued. As previously mentioned, the implementation was fast-tracked. As a result, training did not adequately address user needs, one key user element—published reports—was not implemented, and bugs in the system caused data to appear to be lost on certain input templates during the first two weeks of going live.

With such a poor beginning, Finance has been fighting an uphill battle internally. While adoption has since improved and confidence in the numbers has been restored, many view this system as a burden and don't see its value to them. Instead they see it as a tool to help Finance do its job.

Because users were struggling with the system, Finance formed a Financial Services Group with the charter of providing "cradle to grave" financial services, particularly including use of the new system. However, some business users view

(Continued)

---

[25]*Jean-Michel Cousteau: Ocean Adventures,* one of KQED's nationally produced programs.

this group with suspicion as well, expanding the cultural gap. Says Don Derheim, Executive Vice President of Marketing and Communications, "It's a bit of a struggle between making a sale, raising the money, counting the money, recounting the money, have finance count the money and then make sure you counted it right so that it can come out on March 31st as the number that it was when you counted it way back here."

"For years and years we managed the budget to plus and rarely minus one percent of expense and revenue and now we're asked to still get to that state of excellence but do it in a different way," adds Derheim.

Nemy says that budget variances on major line items have been much larger than plus or minus one percent, and sometimes translate to hundreds of thousands and even millions of dollars.

Other modest improvements in transparency include a new set of management meetings that occur each day, week, and month. This has improved communications within senior management across the multiple functions. According to Traci Eckels, Chief Development Officer, "We have morning 'check-ins' where we tell each other what we're doing. The check-ins are one of the best things for transparency because I find out things I didn't know about, for example, one of our senior staff might be meeting with a donor. At least now I hear about it in the morning with enough time to say, 'Wait, please say this,' or 'I should come with you.' I don't know if the other senior staff like them as much but I think they've been great for transparency."

Another important project also has had some positive impact within the content side of the organization. Delivering *Quest*, which is a multiplatform series, also happens to require a cross-departmental effort. As a part of the process of creating *Quest,* professionals and management (reluctantly) were forced to become a single organization, in support of the *Quest* charter. Although painful at first, the *Quest* team is now fully integrated, is functioning well, and serves as an example of how the rest of KQED may work in the future.

Early signs suggest this is having an influence upon the organization and culture of KQED. In the midst of evaluating a new traffic system, for example, KQED has decided to select one that will manage underwriting inventory for all media types, including radio and TV. In the past each would have insisted on its own system—and gotten it.

While modest progress toward greater transparency has been made, accountability is still quite limited. It is rare that anyone is disciplined for missing objectives. Compliance with initiatives seemingly can be argued with or simply ignored. According to one senior manager, "There aren't consequences for the person who is not carrying their weight, who should not be at the table anymore."

In spite of its significant early shortcomings, the budgeting and forecasting system has been useful in helping the organization understand its budget, run rate, and forecast, and in controlling expenses and taking quick corrective action. This moves KQED from a 2006 score of Chaos Reigns to the midpoint of Departmental Optimization. As some of these initiatives continue to mature, it is possible that this score will improve in the coming years. Strong and definitive commitment by senior management—especially the CEO—will accelerate progress. However, the organizational "hangover" from the system will make future efforts more difficult and will hamper Nemy's ability to serve as its evangelist.

(Continued)

Action on Insights

With the exception of financial budgeting and forecasting systems, any action on insights at KQED has been stuck at the departmental level. As cited before, Marketing and Development have their sources, which are used to benchmark and optimize membership contributions and fundraising activities. Syndicated sources (Arbitron and Nielsen) are analyzed, when available, and are used to influence the timing and quantity of membership drives and, perhaps, the content of programming.

Here too, the financial budgeting, forecasting, and reporting systems represent the only enterprise-wide vehicle for developing insights and (in theory) acting on them. By way of an example, in 2007 KQED was able to identify a budget shortfall in time to cut expenses and increase pledge days. As a result, it was able to contain the shortfall without any negative impact on the organization. For these achievements, KQED ranks at the top of Departmental Optimization for action on insights.

Several managers shared with us the intent to develop a comprehensive management "dashboard" that will include important metrics from across the business—including financial metrics. While an encouraging sign, it isn't clear (to anyone) who would own this initiative. Additionally, costs associated with such a project might be off-putting for a zero-based budget organization such as KQED. Nevertheless, if KQED is able to develop a more comprehensive approach to Business Intelligence and performance management—which this project will require—it inevitably would lead to improved action on insight (and transparency).

Conflict Resolution

From the outside looking in, at core of the KQED culture is a desire to "get along" and "be nice." According to one manager, "I think we all spend a lot of energy trying to get along, so it's hard when there's a real conflict because if you address it, then everybody who knows about it thinks you weren't being nice."

As a result, conflicts often are hidden, with some veteran employees going to the CEO instead of addressing issues and compromising directly with peers. Others simply ignore lingering issues, hoping they'll go away, or they engage in passive-aggressive behavior—pursuing divergent and conflicting paths.

Once again, there are some indications that this may be changing. Although senior management is more consensus-driven, regular meetings provide a forum for airing conflicts. According to Traci Eckels, "I'm not sure we've changed our behaviors all that much. However, now that we have all these meetings, it's much more likely that problems will come up. So, I think we are spending more time talking about things that, in the past, would have stayed in the background and not been resolved."

And, projects such as *Quest* create a new high-water mark for resolving differences and collaborating. While the new budgeting and forecasting system creates conflict, it also enforces resolution. As a result, I rank KQED at the upper end of Departmental Optimization for conflict resolution. This is an improvement over 2006 when it would have been considered bordering on Chaos Reigns. Dramatic and rapid improvement in this category will require the focus of senior management—especially the CEO—who must set the tone for the organization.

Common Trust in Data

Although there remain "stovepipes" of data throughout KQED, people generally trust their data and use it for

(Continued)

various purposes. In 2006, this would have placed KQED in the Departmental Optimization category for common trust in data. The initial fast-tracked implementation of the enterprise-wide budgeting, forecasting, and reporting system caused some regression in this category during 2007. However, since that time, things have improved and this (sole) enterprise-wide source has caused a solid increase in common trust. As a result, its ranking has improved, placing the organization squarely between Performance-Directed Culture Emerging and Departmental Optimization.

And, as we would expect at this level of achievement, users have found ways to manipulate the system to their advantage—using it as a system to "request" funding and "padding" budgets rather than candidly documenting investments and forecasting expected performance.

As stovepipes begin to further break down—through activities such as the upcoming management dashboard, *Quest* influence, and a common traffic system for television and radio—it's possible that KQED again will experience regression since combining and reconciling data from discrete systems is far harder than implementing a wholly new financial system. This regression is natural and to be expected. And, assuming the effort is managed properly, the result should, eventually, be a much higher score.

Availability and Currency of Information

With the exception of the financial reporting system, access to information is extremely limited and is still somewhat restricted to departmental use. Much of the information is not online and is available only in hard copy or extracts from various syndicated sources. According to one employee, "It's actually difficult to get the ratings data out of people around here. You have to find out who has the Nielson data or the

Arbitron data. Then getting them to share it is not easy. When that happens, it signals to me that it's 'dangerous territory'; they're holding it close. What we expose is current but some of it's buried under people's workstations."

Prior to the implementation of the financial budgeting, forecasting, and reporting system, KQED's ranking would have been considered Chaos Reigns. Since the implementation of the system, its score has improved and is now at the top of the departmental optimization category. Should KQED succeed with its intended management dashboard project, this would dramatically improve its score for availability and currency of information.

KQED is a fascinating organization and one that shines within its industry for superior content and support of its constituencies. However, as a performance-directed culture, it is immature. And, while it has made modest progress toward that goal, it lacks clear direction and a sense of urgency.

While management's effort to modernize its budgeting and forecasting systems was certainly needed and has improved fiscal control and increased predictability, it also has alienated many of its business and creative staff. As one employee suggested, it might have been better to start with a solution supporting KQED's core mission first and one for its fiscal control second. As a result, the Finance-led budgeting and forecasting effort has left the business feeling a bit wary about future performance measurement and management initiatives.

On a more positive note, *Quest* and other cross-functional efforts may serve as a "touchstone" for the "new" KQED, but can do so only with deliberate support from management. And, the often-mentioned management dashboard

(Continued)

project needs clear ownership. If it comes to fruition, it may serve as an important forcing function—increasing needed transparency and accountability within KQED.

And finally, refocusing and broadening its performance management efforts to support KQED's mission first, with convincing support from management, certainly would help.

CHAPTER 5

Mueller Inc.

The Central West Texas town of Ballinger, population 4,000, was established by the Santa Fe Railroad in 1886. Named after a railroad attorney who died without ever visiting, it is primarily an agricultural community with some light industry. On the hour-long drive to Ballinger from San Angelo—where the nearest commercial jet airport is located—miles of brown farm and ranch lands testify to the driest winter since records were started in 1895. The U.S. Drought Monitor[1] estimated that the impact on agriculture in the area of the extremely dry weather that began in 2008 had reached more than $1 billion by early 2009.

Still, Ballinger's cost of living in early 2009 was about a third less than the U.S. average, and the unemployment rate in Runnels County—of which Ballinger is the county seat—was about three percentage points lower than the rest of the country. And, while it may seem an unlikely place to find an exemplar of a company with a performance-directed culture, that's exactly what you'll find in Ballinger, headquarters to Mueller Inc.

---

[1] U.S. Drought Monitor is a service of the National Drought Mitigation Center and the University of Nebraska–Lincoln, http://drought.unl.edu/dm/.

Ballinger's largest employer, Mueller traces its origins back to the 1930s when sheet metal worker Walter Mueller started making water cisterns for local farmers and ranchers. When they came of age, Walter's sons, Harold and James, joined the business and over time expanded the company to make other products out of sheet metal,[2] including windmills.

In the 1960s, Mueller began buying secondary steel—steel that has been rejected because it does not meet its original specifications—and built a rolling mill where it fabricated secondary for specific uses.

Secondary steel turned out to be a great business. Steel mills needed to sell it, but their existing customers were not interested because they needed prime quality. Buyers with lower quality requirements wanted it because it was less expensive than prime. So Mueller was able buy secondary cheaply, roll it, and sell it at a huge markup to customers who were happy because the price they were paying was a lot less than the alternatives. Mueller quickly became known as "the bargain yard of the Southwest," with customers from all over Central West Texas coming to Ballinger to buy from Mueller. By 1970, the company was generating $1 million in annual revenue.

Another big breakthrough for Mueller came when the company started to take advantage of a growing trend in the steel building industry, which was to paint steel before rolling it instead of rolling it first and then painting it. The advantages to pre-painting were less time, less hassle, and lower cost compared with painting steel in the field.

The problem—which was the opportunity for Mueller—was that the technology first used to pre-paint steel was new and

---

[2]Sheet metal is metal that is formed into thin, flat pieces that can be cut and bent into different shapes. Because of its strength and reliability, sheet metal is used in countless everyday applications.

early coaters weren't very good at it, producing a lot of secondary. Similar to its original secondary business, Mueller was able to buy pre-painted secondary at a low price, roll it, and, as before, sell it at a huge profit. By the early 1980s, Mueller had grown to $32 million in annual revenue.

New Owners and a Changing Market Demand a New Focus

In 1984, Mueller attracted the attention of the Burly Corporation, a privately held Texas supplier of agricultural fence products owned by the Davenport family. Burly acquired Mueller from the Mueller brothers, and one of the Davenport brothers, Bryan, became President.

By the mid-1980s, though, the U.S. steel industry was in turmoil. It had lost much of its global competitiveness, with technological breakthroughs being made elsewhere and other countries learning to make steel better and more efficiently. One of the ways the industry responded to these pressures was to improve its own quality and efficiency, which led to a dramatic decrease in the availability of secondary. With Mueller's business strategy entirely dependent on being able to buy secondary readily and cheaply, Davenport soon realized it was time to consider a new direction for the company.

"The chicken that laid the golden egg had died," says Davenport. "I knew we had to develop new business opportunities without getting too far away from what we were good at."

What Mueller was good at was sheet metal. But with the secondary market drying up, Mueller had to find a more plentiful supply of steel and that meant prime. Davenport knew that this change was going to be a challenge—Mueller had never had to price and sell a fully costed product. "Believe me, if I could have continued to sell secondary at a generous profit, we wouldn't have made the switch," he says. "But we had no choice."

In addition to sheet metal, another core competency that Davenport didn't want to change was the company's focus on end-user customers instead of contractors, which was the norm in the industry. Mueller's customers were the people who owned the buildings and other projects that Mueller's sheet metal products went into—primarily farmers, ranchers, and other agricultural people living in rural areas. They were hardworking, self-sufficient, and, above all, thrifty people who often preferred to build their own projects—especially when the alternative was to hire an expensive contractor.

Davenport believed that Mueller's focus on the end-user customer was so ingrained in the company that it would be difficult to change. It also was potentially a competitive advantage over companies that worked only with contractors. So even as the company was moving into a different direction with its sheet metal business, Davenport decided to continue serving end users.

Davenport knew that this would be especially challenging. Mueller was known as the low-cost supplier of sheet metal—a position in the market that would disappear rapidly once the company was selling products made of prime. The question was how to retain customers who were motivated primarily by price when Mueller could no longer offer bargain basement prices.

Davenport's answer was to transform Mueller's value proposition from "lowest cost" to "total value."

Of this decision, Davenport says, "It took some time and effort to get that position really solidified in the organization. For example, one of our trucks might go out with 95 percent of the parts a customer was expecting and the driver would say, 'We'll bring the rest of the parts out tomorrow or the next day.' But if you're a total value supplier, that's not okay. You may be giving the customer a cheap price on the parts, but if you're going to cost him two days of down time, that's expensive. There was a quite a bit of reorientation that had to go on around here as to exactly what we were trying to accomplish."

To further deliver on Mueller's total value promise, Davenport also decided to open retail and distribution centers closer to its customers. When Burly acquired Mueller in 1984, one of the first things Davenport did was survey its customers, asking them what they liked and disliked about Mueller. The most common complaint was that customers didn't want to drive all the way to Ballinger to buy from Mueller. Davenport moved slowly at first, opening Mueller's first branch office in 1988. By the early 1990s, Mueller had three branch offices.

Another element of delivering on Davenport's vision of Mueller as a total value supplier was to expand its product offerings. This was based on the assumption that if the company had to increase prices because its materials cost had gone up, it had to offer its customers something that was worth the extra money. So Mueller started putting together steel building "kits"—prefabricated assemblies, subassemblies, and components packaged together that could be assembled on-site to complete buildings. Customers could still build the buildings themselves, but they wouldn't have to drive all over the area to multiple suppliers to get the parts they needed.

Mueller Gets Back on Track

The actions Davenport took in response to the collapse of the secondary market in the mid-1980s enabled the company to continue its growth and success into the early 1990s.

For starters, the decision to offer steel building kits, also known as systems, was a good one. Prefabricated steel buildings had been growing steadily in popularity because of their cost-effectiveness and potential for quick order-to-delivery times. The

1990s turned out to be a period of major growth in the entire industry that has extended into the 2000s. Today, steel building systems are a multibillion-dollar industry[3]; Mueller estimates that its own segment of the industry is probably a $2.5 billion market on its own.

The decision to maintain its focus on end-user customers also paid off, although at the time it was a bold step and to this day remains unusual in the steel building systems industry. Most manufacturers in the industry sell to professional contractors who get contracts with end-user customers, purchase the systems, and then build the buildings. The contractors own the customer relationships, and the manufacturers stay in the background supporting them. Mueller is an exception. While the company doesn't turn contractors away, it still prefers to sell directly to end-user customers.

But perhaps Davenport's most difficult challenge during the transition was repositioning the company from a low-cost supplier to a total value supplier. He struggled with it for several years before realizing that in all its years in business, Mueller had never given its employees a common mission. He tells the story of a traffic manager at Mueller who been with the company for a long time—long before Burly acquired it and Davenport took over. He was an ex-military sergeant set in his ways, and Mueller salesmen would have to negotiate with him—some would say beg him—to schedule deliveries to customers.

"I finally realized that he thought his mission was to bring material in, not send it out," says Davenport. "That's what he'd

---

[3]Like many industries, the steel building industry is taking a hit in the current economy. But the popularity of its products is strong and getting stronger, and a rebound after the recession ends seems assured.

been hired to do and he viewed customer deliveries as getting in the way of doing his job. So one day I went to him and said, 'We're going to change your mission. From now on, your mission is to get material out to the customer. When it's convenient, you can bring material in.'"

According to Davenport, things got a lot better with the traffic manager after that. But the bigger lesson for him was that the only way to get an entire company to focus on a common mission is to articulate it, live it, and communicate it frequently. It's also essential that every individual understand it and his own role in supporting it. It was a practice Davenport adopted then and continues to this day.

And, more than 20 years later—while some of the words have changed—Mueller's mission is still to provide "the best total value to end users" of its products. The difference is that Davenport is confident now that the majority of employees at Mueller understand it—an assertion backed up by the company's most recent annual employee survey.

"They would probably articulate it a little differently," says Davenport. "If they're in the prefab shop, they might say it's important that the project gets out on time and that all the parts fit together. If they're in the call center, they might say it's important that someone answers the customer's question right away. But they know what their job is in supporting the overall company mission."

Even now, though, Davenport acknowledges it's not always easy to stay on track with Mueller's mission, and doing so requires constant vigilance. "We get tugged as much as anybody, and it generally comes up through sales," he says. "They'll have a customer who wants something and they'll have all kinds of reasons why we should give it to them, even if it means new products and more investment. But we're very tenacious about it. We're going to do what we do, and we aren't going to go chasing after the setting sun."

Growth Tests Mueller

By 1993, it was clear that Mueller had made it through the worst of the transition from sheet metal products made from secondary to products made from prime—and all the challenges that came with that shift. But the company's growth and geographic expansion had taken a toll, straining Mueller's management structure, its business processes, and the systems used to run the company.

For example, the management team at Mueller still consisted of just two people: Davenport and John Jones, who was the company's Chief Financial Officer. Jones was a consultant who had worked with Davenport through the acquisition of Mueller, and after its completion, joined the company full time. Davenport was responsible for vision and strategy, sales, and operations, while Jones took care of all the support functions of the company and also played a strong role in any aspect of the company that had a financial impact. Those who knew Jones say he was a tireless worker completely dedicated to the company and instrumental to its success, but also a taskmaster and not comfortable with delegation. Davenport or Jones or the two men together made virtually all of the decisions in the company, no matter how small. By Davenport's own admission, it was an environment in which "employees expected to be given direction."

As for business processes at Mueller, they had been established long before Davenport and Jones arrived at the company and had evolved—or not, as the case might be—without much thought given to scalability.

Lynn Becker, now a Regional Manager at Mueller who joined the company as a salesman in 1985, gives this example: "For a salesman to process an order back then, you had to go out back to the warehouse, find the material, and put your tag on it, which meant you were reserving it. Then you had to hope that another salesman wouldn't take the tag off and reserve it for himself—or that the yard manager wouldn't remove the tag and put someone else's on it because that guy had bought him a beer and you hadn't."

In a nod to efficiency, Mueller had bicycles that the salesmen used to make the trip from the sales office to the warehouse to save time.

As Mueller opened its first branch offices, it became clear to Davenport that the company's manual processes and systems were not up to the task. It was also clear that if the company continued to grow and expand geographically, it was going to be even harder to ensure that everyone in the company stayed focused on the mission. "I knew that the human error involved in all of these manual systems we had was going to create failures in our efforts to take care of our customers," says Davenport.

Despite not having a technology background or much previous experience with it, Davenport decided that technology was the answer to the problem. "I didn't know that technology was the solution, but I was certainly hoping that technology was the solution," he says.

And so, in 1993, Mueller bought its first-ever computer and a financial software package with the intent of automating the company's key business functions. Shortly thereafter, consultants from a large computer systems supplier—the same one that had sold Mueller its computer system—persuaded Davenport to hire them to take a small group of key people in the company through an exercise of reengineering its business processes.[4]

---

[4]For historical context, 1993 was the height of popularity for business process reengineering (BPR), a term coined for an approach advocated by MIT computer science professor Michael Hammer, Ernst & Young consultant Thomas Davenport (no relation to Mueller CEO Bryan Davenport), and others. The premise of BPR was that companies should reengineer their business processes before automating them instead of automating existing ones.

Davenport credits the exercise not just with helping the company improve its processes, but also with putting in place the foundation for a new management structure. "Before that, people got hired and they got paid to do their jobs, but nobody would stick their neck out and make a decision because that was considered dangerous," says Davenport. "The process reengineering project engaged people in a way that we hadn't done before. So we used it to define and solidify some new manager responsibilities."

It took awhile for people to understand and accept their new responsibilities, and one of the things Davenport had to do was make it clear that he was going to back people up when they made decisions. But it was during this time that the seeds of a modern management system at Mueller were planted, and for the first time people in the company were encouraged to work as a team to come up with solutions to address issues and opportunities.

The 21st Century Brings a New Set of Challenges

The process initiatives, technology, and management initiatives Mueller implemented propelled the company through much of the rest of the 1990s by improving its business around the mission of delivering total value to customers. This involved everything from putting in place streamlined processes to ensure that customer deliveries were on time and that its building systems performed as expected—"the low-hanging fruit," says Davenport to improving its existing products and entering new markets.

For example, the company expanded its offerings to include steel building systems that were pre-engineered, meaning designed to meet local building regulations and codes. This enabled Mueller to expand its customer base beyond self-sufficient agricultural people in rural areas to customers in towns and cities looking to build garages and backyard buildings for equipment and recreational storage.

Mueller's revenue growth and geographic expansion continued as well. By 1999, Mueller had achieved $105 million in annual sales and had 11 branch offices. But as before, with growth came new challenges and new complexity. Never one to take success for granted—and always looking ahead—Davenport became concerned that Mueller's computer and software systems were out of date. Mueller's financial software was really just an accounting package that the company used for order processing and general ledger. And, even though the company's manufacturing and distribution processes had been reengineered, the systems used to manage them were still largely manual.

The company's technology lagged in other areas as well. Phillip Arp, a technology industry veteran who joined the company's Finance department in 2000 and is now Chief Financial Officer, describes it this way: "Coming from the technology industry, I get here, got handed a laptop, and I said, 'Fantastic, is it linked up to the network?' Turns out Mueller didn't have a network. If you wanted email, you had to go out and get your own dial-up account. I thought, 'Man alive, this is going to be tough.'"

It was around this time that then-CFO John Jones came to Evanet Gallant, Mueller's IT manager, and told her that Mueller was going to implement an Enterprise Resource Planning (ERP) system, upgrade its computers, and make other technology improvements. Gallant—who joined Mueller 39 years ago as a file clerk and worked her way up to a spot on the management team—says, "John told me that Bryan was concerned that technology was leaving us behind. So we started looking for an ERP system, bought one in October 2000, and got to work."

Adds Davenport, "It wasn't just about technology. I knew that doing that in and of itself wasn't going to add any value. It was about achieving our mission."

Much to everyone's dismay—and no one's more than Davenport—the project took three years to complete and eventually cost Mueller $10 million. Looking back, Davenport says the problem was that Mueller took on too much all at once, deciding to implement all the components of its ERP system—accounting, order entry, manufacturing, distribution—in one big "Go Live."

"It was a pretty trying time," says Davenport. "We came close to a total meltdown a couple of times."

Gallant remembers a moment when she was sitting in her office, exhausted and tired, and Davenport walked in. She looked at him and said, "Bryan, I don't think we're going to make it." He looked back at her and said, "Evanet, we're going to make it. We just need to hang in there together."

As he turned to walk out the door, the phone rang and it was a Mueller employee calling with a problem with the system. As Davenport paused in the doorway, Gallant said to the frustrated caller, "We're going to make it. We just need to hang in there together."

"I'll never forget that," says Gallant. "It says a lot about Bryan and the culture of this company."

Of the overall experience, Davenport says wryly, "I'm glad we did it. But if I had known how long it would take and how much it would cost, I would have never done it willingly."

Mueller's arduous ERP implementation was just one element of a "perfect storm" of external and internal challenges facing the company at the turn of the 21st century.

Among Mueller's external challenges:

- The "steel crisis" of 1999–2001, during which more than 30 U.S. steel producers and processing firms fell into bankruptcy as a result of global excess capacity, forcing the company to add new overseas suppliers to its supply chain

- The rise of China as first a major consumer and then a producer of steel
- Volatility in the prices of raw materials
- Changing customer demographics as uses for steel buildings expanded from primarily farms and ranches to backyard storage and commercial buildings
- New competitors and new approaches to meeting customer needs
- The increasing incidence of drought conditions in the geographic markets served by the company, which placed severe financial pressures on the company's customers

Adding to these external challenges were internal ones:

- The need to maintain good working relationships and ultimately partner with contractors to sell effectively to new types of end users who were less self-sufficient than Mueller's historical customer base
- The need to change product mix and focus due to changing customer demographics
- The decision to accelerate geographic expansion plans and open new branch offices
- The lengthy, expensive, and disruptive ERP system implementation, already described
- The decision of CFO John Jones to retire, which he did in 2002

Much as it had done in the late 1980s when the secondary market dried up, Mueller addressed these new issues and opportunities through a combination of improved processes, more advanced technology, and new management approaches. And, much as it had done in the late 1980s, Mueller developed its strategies while staying true to its mission of delivering total value to end users of its products.

For example, in anticipation of John Jones's retirement, Mueller added two key people to its Finance team in 2000: Phillip Arp, who would become CFO when Jones retired, and Mark Lack, who joined Mueller as Manager of Financial Planning and Analysis.

Formalizing Performance Management at Mueller

As Mueller grappled with how to approach its myriad challenges, Arp and Lack suggested adopting the Balanced Scorecard as a performance management tool. Originated by Drs. Robert Kaplan and David Norton, the Balanced Scorecard is a framework that combines nonfinancial measures with financial metrics to give companies a balanced view of their performance. The Balanced Scorecard also has proven valuable as a tool for communicating performance goals and business strategies throughout an organization to ensure alignment.

Lack describes the situation this way: "We were at another crucial point in our history. The competitive landscape was changing. Mueller was changing. Once again, we needed a way to better organize and manage the company if we were to continue our growth."

According to Lack, Davenport embraced the Balanced Scorecard almost immediately, recognizing it as a powerful tool. An analogy that Davenport reportedly uses is that the Balanced Scorecard allows Mueller's "ship to navigate through the changing waters, past other ships, and steer clear of icebergs the second it sees them on the horizon."

The first step in using the Balanced Scorecard as a performance management and communications tool was to refine the articulation of Mueller's mission—not the mission, which had remained constant since the 1980s, but how it could be described and presented to employees (see Figure 5.1).

Mueller Business Purpose Statement

Mueller's purpose is to deliver the best total value to end users of metal building and residential metal roofing products, in the Central and Southwestern United States.

Mueller's strategy is to directly manage the customer relationship by providing convenient access, reliable products, dependable services, and total solutions at the lowest total cost funded through operating efficiency improvements.

Mueller will limit expansion to the company's ability to effectively manage and finance from retained earnings.

To execute Mueller's purpose, the organization will be expected to embrace these cultural values:

- Seek continuous improvement
- Demonstrate integrity and professionalism
- Manage relationships on the basis of what's right, rather than who's right
- Maintain a high awareness of the total market environment
- Make decisions by selecting the best of all available alternatives
- Measure performance by results and the methods used

The accomplishment of Mueller's purpose will produce sustainable growth and a superior investment return.

FIGURE 5.1   Mueller's Revised Business Purpose Statement

Among other things, the revised Business Purpose Statement crisply articulated Mueller's strategy for achieving the "best total value" as "directly manag[ing] the customer relationship by providing convenient access, reliable products, dependable services, and total solutions at the lowest total cost."

According to Lack, convenient access translates into geographic expansion that brings Mueller closer to customers through new branch offices; reliable products result from automating manufacturing processes and controls to improve quality and consistency; dependable services serve as a rallying cry to all Mueller employees to put front and center getting customers what they need when they need it; and total solutions mean delivering value-added services such as design, engineering, installation support through a contractor network, and even help with financing when customers need it.

After refining its Business Purpose Statement, Mueller's next step was to create a strategy map, a one-page diagram used in the Balanced Scorecard methodology to describe how an organization creates value by connecting strategic financial, customer, process, and learning and growth objectives to one another in a cause-and-effect relationship. Presenting key strategies and their interdependencies on a single page turns the strategy map into an effective communications tool for getting buy-in and alignment throughout an organization.

Mueller completed its strategy map in 2002, created its Balanced Scorecard in 2003, and began cascading the Balanced Scorecard to business and support units in 2004 (see Figure 5.2). It also began using it in management meetings.

By all accounts, Mueller began to see benefits almost immediately. Processes were improved and made more efficient; employees made behavioral changes and were eager to improve wherever they could.

The hard benefits of increased return on assets and sales came later, when Mueller had matured in its use of the Balanced Scorecard. In 2005, the company tied the Balanced Scorecard to budgeting and, in 2006, linked it to compensation and development plans.

An ongoing benefit of the Balanced Scorecard is the clarity it provides. As Lack says, "The Balanced Scorecard makes it easier to spot areas for improvement, keep focused on goals, and measure our performance and progress."

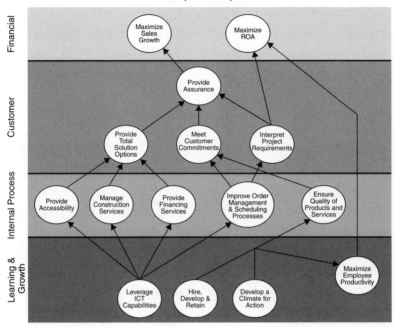

FIGURE 5.2 Managing Performance with the Balanced Scorecard

An ERP System That Works!

In February 2003, in the middle of creating its Balanced Score-card, Mueller was finally ready to "Go Live" with its ERP system. Despite all the problems—and even though it took another year to fully deploy to everyone's satisfaction—its benefits were immediate and obvious, and included some that were unintended.

Says Arp, "Yes, of course the ERP system automated key functions in the company, but it wasn't just about automation. The other thing it did was help enforce a management structure. Everyone had a job to do and because the system tied everything together, you had to do your job so others could do theirs.

"We also had to start communicating better with one another about things before we did them," says Arp. "For example, purchasing might make a decision, change the system, and all of a sudden it would ripple throughout the entire organization. With everyone so interconnected, we all had to work together to make it a success."

Says Davenport, "What developed was a whole new attitude of cooperation, which was hugely important to the organization."

Another benefit to the organization was that many people in the company went into the ERP project with very little experience and a lot of fear about technology, and came out of it with confidence. "Nowadays when we start a project, it's a given that we'll look at how technology can help," says Davenport. "In fact, if you ask me when I declared victory with our ERP implementation, it was when I realized that Mueller was a company that embraced technology and that people here are constantly trying to figure out how to apply it in new areas to improve the business."

Today, of Mueller's 600-plus employees, 350 are direct users of the ERP system and most of the rest are indirect users using wireless handheld devices to collect data that feeds into the system. Says Gallant—with a smile—"We've gone from bicycles to wireless handheld devices. I think $10 million is a bargain."

Beyond ERP to Business Intelligence

Mueller's embrace of technology continued beyond the implementation of its ERP system. Once the ERP system was in place, reporting and business analytics became the next top technology priority—both for managing the company's overall performance and for managing Mueller's growing number of branch offices.

"I'm a big believer in standardization," says Davenport. "But as we added branch offices, every one of them started to look a little different. Before we got too big, I wanted to adopt a set of best practices that we could use indefinitely and anywhere in the country to ensure that our branch offices were being well managed by the local managers."

So in 2004, Mueller created what it calls its Branch Target System. The Branch Target System organizes Mueller branches into three groups—Calves, Heifers, and Cows. According to Lack, the system was inspired by the BCG Matrix, the Boston Consulting Group's legendary tool for analyzing business units and product lines by maturity to determine priorities for allocating resources. One of the phases in the BCG Matrix is "cash cows." Says Lack, "We decided to go all the way with the agricultural theme."

The Calves group includes Mueller's newest and youngest branches as well as any branches that are underperforming. Heifers are the midsized branches and medium performers. At the top are the Cows, Mueller's best performers and usually the most mature. The Branch Target System consists of models for each category of branch office that give managers guidance and direction on how their branches should be performing against a number of key financial metrics.

Says Davenport, "We wanted to give our branch managers the responsibility and authority to run their branches like they are independent businesses, but we couldn't have them all going off and creating their own targets and systems for measuring performance. That might work when you have five branches, but what about when you have 50?"

So branch managers are trained to use the Branch Target System to understand how they should be performing and then they are given reports of their performance against the key financial metrics in the system.

The reports are critical to the branch managers, but in the early days of using the system, Mueller was producing the reports manually, which was taking longer and requiring more people as Mueller's appetite for data grew. Even worse, for all the time the reports took to produce, Davenport was concerned that they were out of date before they were even distributed.

Motivated primarily by this need to produce more timely reports with less effort, Mueller purchased its first automated reporting system in 2004, later upgrading it to a comprehensive Business Intelligence (BI) software suite in 2006.

Of Mueller's technology journey—from its humble beginnings with the purchase of its first computer in 1993 to the implementation of an advanced BI system in 2006—Arp puts it this way: "I always tell people that when I decided to move back to West Texas, I thought I'd have to work as a bookkeeper in some small company to make a living. Imagine my surprise ending up as the CFO in a company that is as sophisticated in its use of technology as any company I've ever worked in."

Mueller Refines Its Management System

In addition to using the Balanced Scorecard and technology to face down its 21st-century challenges, Davenport also elevated key people into managerial positions and formalized a management system that gives them a greater role in decision making around strategy and problem solving. Today, Davenport has 13 direct reports in nine functional areas—Sales, Operations, Finance, Purchasing, IT, Marketing, Human Resources, Partnerships, and Legal.

For now, it's hard to imagine Mueller without Bryan Davenport. For more than 25 years, he has provided visionary and steady leadership, insisting that, despite changes in just about everything else, Mueller's mission stay the same. The formula clearly has worked; the progress Mueller has made over that span of time—and especially in the past 10 years—is impressive by any measure.

From a $32 million company operating out of a single location in Central West Texas in 1984, Mueller today serves the Central and Southwest United States from 28 retail and distribution centers and three manufacturing locations employing more than 600 people. It has expanded its product offerings from sheet metal made from secondary steel to include steel building systems, residential metal roofing, rolling doors, and value-added services. In addition to its retail locations, the company markets and sells via a telephone call center, catalog, and the Internet.

In addition, Mueller has fully embraced performance management methodologies and used technology to fulfill its mission of delivering total value to the end users of its products. The company continually streamlines and automates business processes, ensures alignment with strategy in every corner of the organization through constant communication, and nurtures a highly motivated workforce.

Financially the company has prospered, reaching annual revenue of approximately $250 million in 2008, a compound annual growth rate of 12.5 percent over the previous year, with a return on net assets of 26 percent and a profit before tax of 18 percent.

As Davenport might say—in his characteristically low-key style—pretty good for a small company in a small town in Central West Texas.

Mueller and the Performance Culture Maturity Model

While it's clear that today Mueller has a performance-directed culture, its path has been evolutionary over 25 years rather than revolutionary. And, while the company has made the greatest progress in its journey over the past 10 years in

(Continued)

particular, it's also during that time that the company experienced its greatest setbacks. This emerges in mapping on my
Performance Culture Maturity Model several defining events
that represent phases at Mueller (see Figure 5.3).

The first phase occurred in 2000 and 2001, when Mueller
decided to purchase and implement an ERP system and
began the process of redefining its management structure
in response to the impending retirement of its long-time
CFO. The second phase began in 2002 and extended through
2003, when Mueller created its strategy map and its Balanced
Scorecard and finally went live with its ERP implementation.
The third phase occurred in 2004 and 2005, when the company's ERP system became stable, its Balanced Scorecard
was cascaded throughout the organization, a Target Branch
System for managing its geographic expansion was created,
and its first automated reporting software was purchased.

The fourth phase took place in a single year, 2006, when
Mueller's next phase of BI was underway, making more
detailed and timely operational reporting more widely available as a complement to the Balanced Scorecard and Target
Branch System initiatives. In that same year, the company's
people, processes, and systems were tested by a very successful acquisition of a rival company—and passed with
flying colors.

The fifth phase started in 2007 and continues to the
present time, marked by the adoption of the Balanced
Scorecard in manufacturing and the company's growing
sophistication in its use of the Balanced Scorecard and BI.

It's worth noting that Mueller is unique in several regards.
First, when the current owner, Bryan Davenport, bought
Mueller in 1984, changes in the market forced him to
almost immediately reevaluate the company's mission and
business strategies. He quickly developed a clear vision

	Alignment with Mission	Transparency and Accountability	Action on Insights	Conflict Resolution	Common Trust in Data	Availability and Currency of Information
Performance-Directed Culture Realized	Actionable and embraced mission—supported, informed, and reinforced by metrics [2009]	General transparency and accountability accepted as cultural tenets	"Closed loop" processes ensure timely, concerted action [2009]	Established and effective mechanisms for resolving conflicts	Data as truth: Common application of data, filters, rules, and semantics [2009]	Currency of metrics/data matches rhythm of business [2009]
Performance-Directed Culture Emerging	Actionable mission [2006] supported by "top-down" metrics [2004]	Limited [2009] transparency and accountability; multiple functions collaborate [2006]	Ad hoc [2006] (informal) action on insights across functions [2004]	When identified, conflicts resolved on an impromptu basis [2009] [2006]	Common data: Provincial views and semantics used to support specific positions [2006]	Enterprise availability, uneven currency of information [2006]
Departmental Optimization	[2002] [2000] Alignment with discrete functional goals, not enterprise mission	[2000] [2004] Fragmented transparency and accountability within discrete functions [2002]	[2000] [2002] Uncoordinated/ parochial action (sometimes at the expense of others)	Appearance of cooperation, [2004] "opportunistic reconciliation" [2000]	[2000] Conflicting, functional views of data cause confusion, [2004] disagreement	Availability and currency [2004] directed by departmental sources [2000]
Chaos Reigns	Mission not actionable, not communicated, and/or not understood	Arbitrary accountability, general opacity	Insights rarely leveraged	Conflicting, redundant, and competing efforts are the norm [2002]	Data and information generally unreliable and distrusted [2002]	Multiple, [2002] inconsistent data sources, conflicting semantics

FIGURE 5.3 Mueller and the Performance Culture Maturity Model™

Source: © 2009 Patent Pending Dresner Advisory Services, LLC

for the company and a new mission. The mission, which Mueller refers to as its business purpose, is to "deliver the best total value to end users" of its products. And, while its product offerings have expanded since then, Mueller's mission has remained the same.

In addition, Davenport has been steadfast in his belief in the strategic value of information systems as a means of improving efficiency and return on assets. According to Davenport, "I had this grand vision of being able to deliver hundreds of thousands of orders correctly and on time, and realized that this wasn't going to work if we were passing manual work orders around the shop. So processes had to be supported by technology for it to work. For us to project ourselves forward and build five branches, let alone 30 or 50 or 500 one day, we had to have robust systems."

Phase I: 2000–2001

Although conscious that the company had outgrown the old management structure and was on the verge of profound change, at this point the management team still consisted of just Davenport as President and John Jones as CFO. There were no other C-level executives, directors, or managers in place.

At the core of strategy, these two men directed all tasks downward to the organization for execution. According to Davenport, "We had this problem where people would look to be given direction. But this was your typical entrepreneurial kind of culture where the owners, in this case, made every decision. If things didn't work right and somebody did take a chance, then it might turn out badly."

Related to my Maturity Model, this placed Mueller at the level of Departmental Optimization across all criteria. Departments, including branches, were run as semiautonomous units. Although the mission was well defined and communicated, alignment was uneven as most employees were focused upon tasks, not goals and objectives. Departments and their employees were predominantly concerned with their own narrow objectives, without much regard for other departments. As a result, conflicts often developed between departments, and jockeying for position with senior management was paramount.

According to Mark Lack, "Manufacturing was concerned with manufacturing. Sales was concerned with sales. We were very fragmented and there was little cooperation. We would come together at the end of a closed quarter and review our performance. In a lot of cases it was three to four months after things happened so it wasn't even really timely. During this time, some people would say, 'Let's break down the walls and let's work on objectives together.' All that meant was, 'I'm going to do my stuff and you had better do your stuff.'"

Phase II: 2002–2003

At this point a new management structure had been defined and staffed, in anticipation of the CFO's retirement. According to Phillip Arp, "The entire organizational structure was fairly rigid with respect to all the processes feeding up to Bryan and John. So you had a rigid structure with rigid processes—planning processes and everything else. That's the way a small company generally is. You have to build those processes in order to do that. They realized that they needed to build a corporate staff because they needed to start preparing for a larger company, so they started hiring."

There was now a distinct IT function, a human resources department, a strategic planning function, a new CFO, and

(Continued)

regional sales managers—all reporting to Davenport. To reinforce the new management structure, prepare for growth,
and continue to improve efficiency and return on assets,
Mueller earlier had decided to implement a far-reaching ERP
system—commencing Mueller's very difficult ERP odyssey.

Mueller had taken on the impossible task of implementing all modules of a new ERP system, in what employees
refer to as the "big bang." A very painful implementation
ensued as Mueller attempted to simultaneously implement
sales order entry, manufacturing, distribution, and accounting. The extreme amount of disruption, time, resources, and
expense was unforeseen and, for a time, Mueller was thrown
into near-chaos. This distracted almost everyone, especially
management, and turned 2002 and part of 2003 into "the lost
year."

As Evanet Gallant says, "We bought it in October 2000;
began implementation the next spring; and it took us until
February of 2003 to 'Go Live.' I think that was the most
painful period in any of our lives."

According to Davenport, "2003 is when we did the big
bang. That is what really baked the whole cake. It was
that fire, and coming out of it, when really all of a sudden
the organization and the management team really matured
because there was no choice. It was a pretty trying time. But
we fought our way through it and managed to get on the
other side."

As a result, this phase is marked by significant regression in transparency and accountability, conflict resolution,
common trust in data, and availability and currency of
information—thrusting Mueller back into the Chaos Reigns
category for those criteria on the Maturity Model. This was
a disheartening time for Mueller. However, to its credit, the
company—and especially Davenport—remained patient and
determined to make it work.

Although nearly overshadowed by the challenges of its ERP implementation, Mueller began to design a Balanced Scorecard system to further support its business mission and strategy. According to Lack, "As we entered this 'chaotic' phase we had a lot of things going on. We were implementing the ERP and we were doing some rudimentary reports. We started to develop the Balanced Scorecard at the time because we were looking for a good way to manage a lot of this. We implemented it a year later."

"During that time period there was rapid change," says Lack. "We were trying to implement and manage the ERP and develop some new models for our management systems at the same time. A lot of this work was going on behind the scenes. The whole company was focused on the ERP implementation. A very small group worked on the Balanced Scorecard. That's why it was a kernel, a seed that was planted in 2002 that didn't start to germinate until 2004. That's when we started to see the growth of some of these initiatives."

Phase III: 2004–2005

At this point the ERP system had become stable enough to be used, and significant amounts of varied business data were now being collected. The ERP system also had the effect of enforcing new roles and responsibilities across the company and reinforcing its mission. During this period, the traditional revenue planning and forecasting process was modified in favor of the Branch Target System, which employed a predetermined expense and resource model for each range of anticipated revenues. This Branch Target System helps management achieve greater efficiency and predictability in its sales model through standardization.

Says Davenport, "We came up with the idea of buckets. If we're operating at this level here's what we should

(Continued)

look like. If we're operating at this level here's what we should look like. So managers who are responsible for headcount, hours of production, and so on, can see what the volumes are. Their objective is just to get it to that level. And that is the level of information we provide. What do you need, to know where you are against your target? Your target is predetermined once a year, sometimes twice, but we've tried to move to a system that affords us a lot of flexibility. This is contrary to the American idea of management, which is, 'By golly, you set a target and you make it happen.' But it works for us."

Mueller also implemented its Balanced Scorecard solution in this phase, managed by Finance. According to Lack, "Alignment with the mission really became much stronger in 2004. It was improved because we were showing people, 'This is what we should be doing.'"

The Balanced Scorecard further articulated the mission, made accountability more plausible, and helped improve Mueller's performance in virtually every category. This was especially true for Alignment with Mission and Action on Insights, which climbed into the Performance-Directed Culture Emerging category. However, key areas of Transparency and Accountability, Conflict Resolution, Common Trust in Data, and Availability and Currency of Information saw only modest improvements in this phase and remained stuck in Departmental Optimization.

This was partly because detailed operational reporting linked to the Balanced Scorecard was not available yet, causing users to make separate requests for information to the IT department. Drawn from operational systems and not the data warehouse, which was under Finance control, the numbers often didn't match those in the Balanced Scorecard.

Nevertheless, this was a period of significant achievement for Mueller and marked the turning point to a performance-directed culture. In Davenport's words, "Today I feel like we're a mature management team. People understand and accept their responsibilities and roles, and we work together as a team. There's no one person that has unnecessary exposure or is going to make critical decisions, but everybody is going to be impacted by somebody else or dependent on somebody else so we try. It's more of a team attitude toward solutions and addressing issues and addressing opportunities than certainly there was 10 years ago and 20 years ago."

Phase IV: 2006

By 2006, the ERP system was functioning well, and its reliability and credibility were well established. All of management relied on the Balanced Scorecard, although it had not yet been cascaded to Manufacturing. Added to this was operational reporting to complement the aggregated views of metrics provided by the Balanced Scorecard. This was especially helpful to Sales, which had become more sophisticated in its use of information, and was asking for more complex reports. With increased confidence and reliance upon its information systems, the Balanced Scorecard and BI systems in place, Mueller's ranking moved up to Performance-Directed Culture Emerging in almost every category.

Its newfound ability to behave as a performance-directed culture and as a single organism was tested during this year as Mueller acquired four new branches from a competitor. To its credit, Mueller was able to absorb these new employees and branches—completely automating them with all of its

(Continued)

systems—in less than two months. Says Lack, "The moment when I was awed with the processes we now have in this company was when we did the acquisition. In literally less than 30 days, we were up and running as the Mueller organization with the signs, employees, computers, and systems in place. And we did all four locations in one day."

Says Davenport, "We worked out what had to be done and everybody took their part. HR was off interviewing and setting up the processes we were going to have to go through to incorporate the employees we wanted to bring on. Accounting was setting up doing all the preparatory work to get ready. We had a ton of work. And it really wasn't a major disruption because again all of these processes were so standardized that it's just a matter of executing it."

Phase V: 2007–2009

During this phase, Mueller continued to refine its systems, expand the number of branches, and become more disciplined in its use of performance management and BI. Continued refinements to the Branch Target System were made and, most recently, Manufacturing adopted the Balanced Scorecard, with a primary focus upon efficiency and reduction of scrap metal—resulting in a significant cost savings.

According to Lack, "We saw an improvement in our management schedule and processes. People now are concerned and ask things like, 'Why is this order sitting here?' and 'What do we need to do to get these orders invoiced?' When we have scrap, they ask, 'What's going on with the scrap? Why is our scrap so high?' People started asking the questions that they couldn't before because they didn't have the information and the understanding of why it was important."

Mueller also continued to improve its rankings on the Maturity Model. Through consistency and determination, Mueller rose to the level of Performance-Directed Culture Realized for Alignment with Mission, Action on Insights, Common Trust in Data, and Availability and Currency of Information.

With a well-established performance-directed culture, and enabling technologies and solutions, Mueller has been able to readily take stock of its capabilities and, in the context of a slowing economy, has been able to make key investments in preparation for the next stage of growth. For example, according to Arp, the company is taking advantage of the decline in real estate pricing to buy land in areas where it would like to open new branch offices in the future. The company also is looking at other investments to make up for the loss in income from operations. Says Arp, "We want to be positioned well, not just sitting around with our cash in a mattress, so that when the market does turn around we are ready."

A final note on Mueller: In most cases, companies engage in performance management initiatives after a "wake-up call" of some sort, either externally or internally driven. Mueller is an exception to this rule. Under Bryan Davenport's leadership, Mueller has moved forward patiently and deliberately, investing heavily, enduring setbacks, but never wavering in its commitment to its core values, its mission, and the fervent ownership of performance improvement initiatives.

CHAPTER 6

Tying It All Together

In this book, I've presented case studies about ordinary companies and their extraordinary struggles and triumphs in establishing performance-directed cultures. Along the way, I have used my Performance Culture Maturity Model (see Figure 6.1) as both a filter and a lens for measuring their progress. Specifically, using six key criteria and four levels of achievement, I've ranked each organization based on its development over time.

While the Maturity Model is a valuable tool for revealing what an organization has achieved, it doesn't tell us why or how it did it or offer insights into how others can achieve similar results. In this chapter, I'll compare and contrast the case studies and present common themes and lessons learned.

It's All about Change

The most striking common theme in organizations seeking to create performance-directed cultures is that their stories are all about change: how to create and foster change; how to manage and sustain change; and how to overcome impediments to it. Think of DHG and its change of ownership and desire for national expansion in 2006; Cleveland Clinic and a CEO faced with financial crises in both the late 1980s and late 1990s; and

	Alignment with Mission	Transparency and Accountability	Action on Insights	Conflict Resolution	Common Trust in Data	Availability and Currency of Information
Performance-Directed Culture Realized	Actionable and embraced mission—supported, informed, and reinforced by metrics	General transparency and accountability accepted as cultural tenets	"Closed loop" processes ensure timely, concerted action	Established and effective mechanisms for resolving conflicts	Data as truth: Common application of data, filters, rules, and semantics	Currency of metrics/data matches rhythm of business
Performance-Directed Culture Emerging	Actionable mission supported by "top-down" metrics	Limited transparency and accountability; multiple functions collaborate	Ad hoc (informal) action on insights across functions	When identified, conflicts resolved on an impromptu basis	Common data: Provincial views and semantics used to support specific positions	Enterprise availability, uneven currency of information
Departmental Optimization	Alignment with discrete functional goals, not enterprise mission	Fragmented transparency and accountability within discrete functions	Uncoordinated/parochial action (sometimes at the expense of others)	Appearance of cooperation, "opportunistic reconciliation"	Conflicting, functional views of data cause confusion, disagreement	Availability and currency directed by departmental sources
Chaos Reigns	Mission not actionable, not communicated, and/or not understood	Arbitrary accountability, general opacity	Insights rarely leveraged	Conflicting, redundant, and competing efforts are the norm	Data and information generally unreliable and distrusted	Multiple, inconsistent data sources, conflicting semantics

FIGURE 6.1 Performance Culture Maturity Model™

Source: © 2009 Patent Pending Dresner Advisory Services, LLC

Mueller reacting to dramatic shifts in its market in the late 1980s and late 1990s. Even at KQED, which has not yet figured out completely how to manage change when it comes to financial and operational performance, the catalyst for its fledging performance management initiative was the desire to create a stronger organization to meet the demands of public broadcasting in a new century.

And, as the case studies demonstrate, the desire or intent to change isn't enough to succeed. A number of other conditions must be present that provide a needed context for that change. These four case studies—both their successes and failures—can be defined by the following necessary conditions, sometimes separately and more often in some combination: visionary leadership, organizational activism, business advocacy, and data literacy.

Visionary Leadership

By visionary leadership, I mean leadership at the most senior levels of the organization—a CEO or other C-level executives who embrace a performance-directed culture (especially transparency and accountability) as a pillar of the organization's business strategy. Truthfully, only executives at this level can substantially impact the organization as a driver, influencer, and enabler. They are also the only individuals in an organization whose impact spans all categories of the Maturity Model. And finally, without commitment at this level of leadership, achievement at the highest level of the Maturity Model is not possible.

As a driver, visionary leaders create structure, issue directives, allocate funding, inject new blood into the organization, and reorganize to accelerate change. They are also important influencers—setting the tone for the organization and communicating what is strategic and critical, and quickly changing attitudes and opinions throughout the organization. And, they are the single most significant enabler within the organization, freeing up needed resources, adding credibility and encouragement to fledgling efforts, and ensuring the cooperation of key resources.

Think of Bryan Davenport at Mueller and his 25-year drive to create a performance-directed culture. While there are many committed and talented people at Mueller helping the company perform at its best, it's Davenport who sets the tone and strategy, and chooses the people he thinks can help the company achieve new and higher levels of growth and success.

Organizational Activism

Just because your organization may not have a C-level executive as enlightened about performance management as Bryan Davenport does not mean you cannot make significant progress as measured by the Maturity Model. You'll just have to go about it in a different way. In many organizations, for example, performance management initiatives begin at the departmental level and are driven by a passionate individual or two within the department. I call these people organizational activists.

Organizational activists are knowledgeable, focused, committed, and persistent in solving the most important problems in an organization—even when there is limited support for what they're doing. Organizational activists can appear anywhere in the organization and can be either appointed by management or self-appointed.

Think of Chris Donovan in Finance and Andrew Proctor in Medical Operations at Cleveland Clinic. The two men started performance management initiatives in their own departments and then pooled their resources and began working together to reach a wider audience within the organization. While they were appointed to their tasks within their own departments—and had the support of their immediate supervisors—they had to reach out first to each other and then to other areas of the organization to promulgate success. This was something they did on their own.

What's interesting to note about Cleveland Clinic is that because Donovan and Proctor began working together under the radar, so to speak, when Dr. Toby Cosgrove became CEO in 2004 and they had the opportunity to show him the work they had done, it was far enough along that Cosgrove immediately understood its value and threw his support behind the effort. In that situation, it took the combination of organizational activism and visionary leadership for the effort to gain momentum within the Clinic. It's possible that without Cosgrove's support, the work eventually would have foundered. It's also possible that without the work done by Donovan and Proctor, it would have taken Cosgrove a lot longer to identify the key elements required to achieve a performance-directed culture.

Business Advocacy

Business advocacy occurs when the business side of the organization (Sales, Marketing, and Operations, for example) embraces a performance-directed culture and eventually enlists the support of top management and IT to provide the management support, processes, and technologies necessary to make performance initiatives work.

Business advocacy—while a powerful force—is fairly rare as a primary catalyst in an organization because that degree of cooperation and collaboration across functions is rare. In fact, in most organizations, divisions, departments, and functions prefer to compete with one another, often protecting redundancy and working at cross-purposes. However, getting all functions to behave as a single organism with a common purpose and in alignment with the mission is paramount to a performance-directed culture.

Developing this sort of advocacy requires a "sea change" in behavior and attitudes—requiring internal organizational activism from within the business (think Cleveland Clinic) or from visionary leadership (think Mueller and also the most recent leadership change at Cleveland Clinic).

Data Literacy

Data literacy occurs when people within an organization develop an understanding and fluency for using data, information, and related insights in the decision-making process. In building a performance-directed culture, data literacy serves as a critical enabler. While it may come about through an IT-driven Business Intelligence (BI) or data warehousing initiative, other sources are also possible. And, in all cases, data literacy and the organizational activists who often foster it offer important enablement, supporting business advocacy and easing the organization's transition to a performance-directed culture.

The best example of data literacy among our case studies is DHG, whose co-CEO Brooke Barrett and CIO John Cahill together decided to hire a BI expert. In the wake of 9/11, however, the value of the data and proficiency of the particular expert DHG hired, caused a revelation within the company, propelling the perceived value and importance of data in decision making and performance management initiatives to new heights.

Other Factors to Consider

It's interesting to note that in two of the four case studies in this book, making progress in one area caused regression in other areas. This is normal and can be caused by a variety of factors, but frequently by a flawed technology implementation. Both DHG and Mueller experienced this sort of setback—Mueller with its ERP system implementation and DHG with the rocky upgrade of its BI system—yet each worked through the issues to create a performance-directed culture. KQED is not as far along as Mueller and DHG in overcoming the setback of an imperfect technology implementation, but there are many reasons to believe that it will.

Another important factor is executive sponsorship, which while not a substitute for visionary leadership, is desirable because it often brings funding and charter. John Cahill, then-CIO of DHG, served as an early sponsor of the performance management initiatives there, which allowed them to begin and then gain momentum of their own. At Cleveland Clinic, departmental executive sponsorship made Donovan and Proctor's early efforts possible until visionary leadership in the form of the Clinic's current CEO emerged.

A third, and often critical, factor—present in two of the four case studies in this book—is the "wake-up call" that energizes management and creates opportunities to advance aspects of a performance-directed culture. The two financial shortfalls at Cleveland Clinic in the 1980s and 1990s led the then-CEO to first initiate Performance Wheels—which were originally for his own use—and then after a second financial crisis to start holding monthly Summits to review performance on the Wheel with the Chairmen of each Clinic department. DHG's wake-up call was clearly 9/11, when leveraging its customer data enabled it to outperform its peers during a time when hotel occupancy in New York City was tanking.

In the cases of Mueller and Cleveland Clinic, management transitions also opened the door to further change. For Mueller, it was the impending departure of its long-time CFO in the early 2000s. At Cleveland Clinic, it was the arrival of Cosgrove in 2004. Wake-up calls and transitions must be recognized for what they are—open doors for change. When properly leveraged, they offer important accelerants for emerging performance-directed cultures.

With these conditions and other factors serving as the framework and context, we can reexamine our four case studies for lessons learned.

DHG: Data Literacy Emerges as Primary Driver of a Performance-Directed Culture

The initial seed for change at DHG was then-CIO John Cahill's efforts in 1999 and 2000 to persuade the owners of the company at the time to hire a BI expert to help them mine the data that the company had been gathering for several years. He was successful in gaining support from one of the partners in particular, Brooke Barrett, and in 2001, the company hired Menka Uttamchandani. Just six months later, 9/11 occurred. Despite her short tenure with the company, Uttamchandani had been able to organize and evaluate the quality of DHG's data. When the company began urgent attempts to analyze data to drive occupancy—and thereby avoid potential disaster—it worked!

Prior to this time, just one or two others in key positions at DHG—one example being the company CMO John Moser—relied on data to drive decision making. But after 9/11 and the company's use of data to chart its recovery, more people saw the value of data and information, and attitudes changed. The BI effort was given increased scope and influence—a huge accelerant—and for the next several years Uttamchandani was empowered to expand the BI program—delivering dashboards to revenue management and other areas—with the tacit support of the owners and active support of the CIO. This had the effect of substantially increasing data literacy at the company.

Looking at its rankings on the Maturity Model at the time, you can see that this is reflected positively in its scores for Common Trust in Data and Availability and Currency of Information. However, it was when DHG's management structure was consolidated from six partners to co-CEOs through a management buyout and recapitalization that strategic changes began to occur. Armed with a new vision, the freshly minted visionary leadership made a conscious decision to change the culture in favor of greater transparency and accountability.

Among other things, top management brought in external management resources and began to decentralize some management functions. The resulting mix of old and new culture and management styles sometimes presented an obstacle to Uttamchandani and her team—forcing them to rethink their approach from a centralized, top-down approach to one that supports a decentralized organization using information to manage and align. As they have adapted to this new structure, the ability to increase business advocacy also has grown.

The Bottom Line for DHG

A strong data literacy program and an external wake-up call (9/11) set the stage for a performance-directed culture, and management's evolution into more visionary leadership firmly established the roadmap for DHG to become a performance-directed culture. DHG's rankings remain strongest on Common Trust in Data and Availability and Currency of Information due to its very successful data literacy program. More recent changes by its leadership have succeeded in elevating its other rankings across the Maturity Model, and DHG is well on its way to a performance-directed culture.

Cleveland Clinic: Performance-Directed Culture Emerges through Organizational Activism

Cleveland Clinic's data literacy had been well established as early as 1995. However, the genesis of its performance-directed culture occurred within its lines of business when Chris Donovan of Finance and Andrew Proctor of Medical Operations joined forces to consolidate their individual performance management initiatives.

Tired of taking "heat" at senior management meetings when they presented contradictory views of performance—and under the radar of management and with limited support from IT—these organizational activists were able to build a series of dashboards that enabled them to combine their views of the business and present a common front to management. As a result, Donovan and Proctor began to develop strong business advocacy and began fielding requests from other departments and divisions to help improve their own performance.

During this time, this cross-departmental initiative was able to single-handedly improve Cleveland Clinic's score dramatically on the Maturity Model, most notably in the areas of Transparency and Accountability, Action on Insights, and Conflict Resolution. Then, when a new visionary leader, Dr. Toby Cosgrove, was appointed CEO, Donovan and Proctor (independently and shrewdly) developed a key application that supported one of Cosgrove's new strategic initiatives—patient access. As a result, Cosgrove became a strong advocate.

With Cosgrove's active support, this cross-functional BI team became the Enterprise BI Group and went on to develop a number of dashboards—including the Institute Scorecard that Cosgrove uses as the basis of managing Institute performance. With all of the other factors now in place (data literacy, business advocacy, and visionary leadership), Cleveland Clinic's rankings on the Maturity Model rose across the board.

The Bottom Line for Cleveland Clinic

With data literacy already well established, the Medical Operations and Finance-driven BI effort, which began as a grassroots movement started by organizational activists, built up a strong following among business users at the Clinic. This allowed it to evolve into an enterprise-wide group once a new CEO was appointed.

KQED: Waiting for a Wake-up Call?

KQED is the least evolved of our four case studies on the Maturity Model. Its CEO, Jeff Clarke, while an industry and business visionary in the public broadcasting space, has not yet fully embraced a performance-directed culture as core to the organization's strategy. And, with a clash of cultures between Finance and the business of KQED, real business advocacy for a performance-directed culture has not yet emerged.

On the plus side, there is a strong respect for and use of data throughout the organization on the media side, and data literacy among its key executives and managers is high. This suggests that the organization could develop equal data literacy on the financial and operational side if and when the cultural divide is bridged.

In addition, there are signs that some organizational activism is present within Finance and it is helping to advance KQED from Chaos Reigns to Departmental Optimization on the Maturity Model.

(Continued)

The Bottom Line for KQED

Currently lacking the conditions for a performance-directed culture—and impeded by a cultural divide between Finance and the lines of business—KQED probably needs some sort of a wake-up call to move to the next levels of maturity as a performance-directed culture. In the absence of such a wake-up call, KQED could make progress by focusing on improving business advocacy or data literacy, or through greater strategic commitment by senior management.

Mueller: Visionary Leadership Drives a Performance-Directed Culture Right from the Start

From the start of his tenure in 1984, CEO Bryan Davenport has been a visionary leader and the driving force behind change and success at Mueller. Although he was sensitive to changes in the marketplace and the organization at every step, the most dramatic shift occurred in 2000, when then-CFO John Jones intended to retire. Up to that point, Davenport and Jones comprised the senior management team and few (if any) of the elements of a performance-directed culture existed or were needed. With a different organization and culture in mind, however, Davenport staffed his new management team and included CFO Phillip Arp and Manager of Planning and Financial Analysis Mark Lack.

Along with Davenport, Arp and Lack formed the core of the performance-directed culture team and served as its key drivers, influencers, and enablers. Although Davenport could have driven change by edict, he instead leveraged his reputation as a respected leader to involve his people in the process. This ensured that the emerging performance initiatives met their needs as well as those of management, and also guaranteed their support from the beginning.

Davenport, Arp, and Lack went on to establish Mueller's Balanced Scorecard, which began driving data literacy and business advocacy simultaneously. As a result, on the Maturity Model, Alignment with Mission emerged before most other criteria. However, once underway, Mueller's Balanced Scorecard effort caused the company's rankings to rise fairly evenly across the board.

The Bottom Line for Mueller

Mueller's visionary CEO first charted its course and set the changes in motion to create a data-driven organization supported by technology. He then actively guided the process of instituting a modern management system through several stages of development, which ultimately culminated in a fully mature performance-directed culture.

Applying the Lessons Learned

In closing, I'd like to offer a few suggestions that may help you apply some of these lessons learned in your own organization.

First, use the Maturity Model to map your own progress and status. Pick several periods that stand out as distinguishable eras or milestones related to creating a performance-directed culture, and then plot your organization as I did with our case studies in the earlier chapters. This will help you paint a picture of your own progress and identify the gaps that are yet to be addressed.

I would suggest that you also have some colleagues in other departments go through this process. You may be surprised to find that their assessment differs from yours. This was my experience in working with many of our case studies. Don't be discouraged to find that you're not as advanced as you want to be or thought you were. Most organizations will find themselves with Departmental Optimization as a "center of gravity."

Second, ask yourself which case study is most like your organization and which conditions for change currently exist that will enable you to begin or accelerate the process of becoming a performance-directed culture. Is it visionary leadership, organizational activism, business advocacy, or data literacy? Most organizations will have at least one of these conditions, and with a newfound understanding of the role they can play in a performance-directed culture, perhaps they can be tapped specifically for this effort. Recognizing your own potential role and how you can collaborate with others to drive a performance initiative, will help. Also be conscious of forces that may work against you, such as cultural discord or competing initiatives.

Third, ask yourself whether there are opportunities for executive sponsorship that can provide a charter and funding to get started. Executive sponsorship often can be found in areas of an organization that faces pressing problems and that has leadership motivated to solve them.

Fourth, be alert to the potential for events or transitions that can serve as a wake-up call for your organization to begin or accelerate a performance initiative. They may not be as dramatic as 9/11 or a CEO transition, but can still be used to rally support within the organization for a performance management initiative. Some possibilities include an economic downturn, a new competitor entering the market, the end-of-life of a flagship product, and changing customer demographics and demands. If leveraged in the right way, even these more routine occurrences can be used to evangelize a change in your organization to more of a performance orientation.

* * *

Armed with the insights provided by these case studies, my hope is that you will apply my Maturity Model as a filter and lens, for your own organization to assess your status and create a roadmap for your own journey into becoming a performance-directed culture.

Best of luck!

Index